The Management of Oil Industry Exploration & Production Data

The Management of Oil Industry Exploration & Production Data

Steve Hawtin

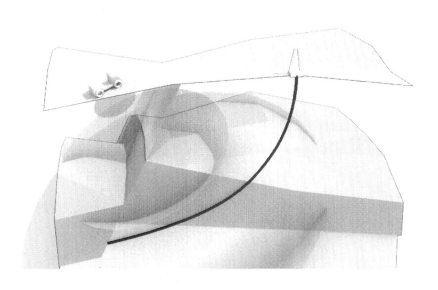

Table of contents

1. Introduction

Oil companies are information based businesses. Those that are best at interpreting measurements and keeping track of what they know about the hidden underground world will succeed, those that aren't, won't. Oil companies are not unique in how much they rely on information, but exploration and production (E&P) is one of the activities where the financial impact of data is highest. In 2011 half of the ten most valuable companies in the world were oil companies[1].

In 2009 DAMA (Data Management International) published the "Data Management Body of Knowledge" (DMBoK) a generic description of the best practices for data management across a wide range of different industries. This 600 page reference work provides a detailed review of the best data handling practices distilled out of the experiences of numerous experts. But the E&P business, like every information based industry, faces its own unique combination of challenges. This document supplements the DAMA book, it provides examples that explore how the principles of DMBoK can be applied in practice to oil industry technical data, it also explores the topics where the DAMA approach has been tried for E&P data in the past and failed.

The most successful data managers must coordinate service delivery, project management, infrastructure deployment, document libraries, relational databases, information architectures and physical asset handling. At the same time they must be able to explain to the users why they should continue to follow the company's standards and procedures and communicate to the budget holders how the money they spend on handling data is delivering value to the business.

---

[1] Based on the "Financial Times Global 500 2011" market values & prices at 31 March 2011

There is a shortage of qualified personnel that have experience running data management activities for E&P companies. This is for two reasons, firstly because academic training in data management is rare, there are plenty of qualified information technologists and computer scientists but few courses that specialize in the actual management of data. Secondly, those that best understand geoscience data are interested in rocks, geological processes and the history of the planet, they usually want to focus on interpreting the subsurface and leave data handling to others.

Good oil industry data managers have mostly learnt their trade on the job, either as computer staff that have had to piece together the way oil company data works from trying to address real issues in a working company, or as geoscientists that have come to realize that the way the data flows has an enormous impact on their organization's financial success. It is hoped that both these communities will find some value in this material.

Acknowledgements

This book is the result of insights from numerous different people collected over the course of many years. In particular I'd like to thank all those countless people that have put up with my awkward questions. Picking out a few names would just emphasize those left out, so instead I'll highlight three key groups: current and ex-colleagues at both Schlumberger and Oilfield Systems; oil company clients; and discussions at various industry gatherings, such as POSC, the Geoshare User's Group, EAGE, AAPG, ECIM, DAMA SMI, and especially Phil Crouse's annual PNEC meeting in Houston. I also like to thank all those that provided valuable feedback for this text. Finally I would like to thank my wife Angela Beasley and our two daughters, Eleanor and Rosalind for their continued support and constructive sarcasm.

2. The value of data to oil companies

The oil industry is an information led business, the market capitalization of companies is mainly dependent on an expectation of the value of future production. This is a number that depends entirely on the interpretation of data about resources that are both hidden far below the earth's surface and are often also in remote and inaccessible locations. The very nature of these resources means that a completely accurate picture is impossible to obtain, the best that can be done is to gather various evidence that informs guesses about future opportunities.

The way these interpretations are handled is one of the main things that differentiate one oil company from another. The company that can anticipate future discoveries and safely develop assets in the most cost effective way will succeed. Organizations that don't do these things will be out-competed and become candidates for future corporate acquisitions.

"Here, you see, it takes all the running you can do, to keep in the same place"

Figure 1: Oil companies have to continually strive to keep relative position[2]

Oil companies are in constant competition, this means that they must continually improve just to maintain their current relative

---

[2] The name Red Queen situation has been applied to this type of dynamic following Matt Ridley's popularization of the term in his book "The Red Queen: Sex and the Evolution of Human Nature"

position. The company that relies on doing things the same way will slip further and further behind. New discoveries are uncovered either by innovating new ways to understand the data, or by applying existing techniques in new regions for the first time.

In all these activities, the data and the way the data is handled, is one of the crucial elements. Yet, for whatever reasons, there are no oil companies that recognize their information as an asset in their annual accounts.

Why measure value?

There are some within oil companies that claim data has no inherent value. Their view is that because the people and infrastructure are required to make sense of any data it has no value in itself. This seems like a perverse view, the fact that a good omelette needs a chef does not mean that the freshness of the eggs is unimportant.

Assigning a value to the data that an oil company holds is important for a number of reasons. For example, all data has a cost to acquire, whether this must be spent with an external contractor to take some measurement or hiring internal experts to interpret a range of inputs. Unless there is some "value" in holding data how can anyone decide how much to spend to obtain it?

Measuring costs

Information is such an important element within the modern oil company that one would have thought the costs of handling it would be precisely documented. This is, however, almost never the case.

It is, of course, difficult to measure the costs of such a pervasive activity. In addition, there is some experience that illustrates how apparently rational decisions can make this even more challenging. A few years ago a major oil company decided that data management should be cheaper so, rather than buying expensive services from a specialized provider, they decided to put the task out for bids from off-shore companies. Of course they did this through their procurement department, who didn't fully understand all the activities being carried out and so specified a list of services that didn't completely match what was required. The procurement process focused on locating the lowest cost bidder, who obviously had to aggressively cut costs in order to out-compete their rivals. When the service was rolled out the users quickly identified things that needed to be done which had not been included. The low cost bidder could not just extend the service, their margins had been shaved thin enough already. The users found that they had to hire additional staff to perform these now "extra" tasks. But now they had a problem, if these new resources were called "data management" then it would be obvious that the exercise of off-shoring had actually increased total costs, which would be bad for the senior executive who had sponsored the whole project. So these new people were labeled as "secretarial staff", or "junior geophysicists", or indeed as anything other than "data managers".

This type of perverse incentive to obscure the real activities is encountered in many organizations.

Measuring value

The "International Valuation Standards Council"[3] suggests that there are three ways to set a value for an intangible asset:

- **Direct market comparison:** identify a "market" where an equivalent is available and use it to estimate a fair price
- **Profit:** Identify the current and future benefit that the company derives from the asset, and use that to estimate a level of investment that would deliver an equivalent yield

---

[3]"International Valuation Standards Council" is a body set up to ensure that consistent standards are applied for inclusion in financial statements, whether for regulatory compliance or to support secured lending and transactional activity. Their standard IVS 301.02 describes how to estimate the value of intangible assets.

- **Cost:** Identify the complete cost to acquire, maintain and if necessary replace the asset

The most reliable estimates of the value of intangible assets would come from the price paid in an open market to obtain it. However, while petrotechnical data may be included as part of a company acquisition or a farm-in, this almost inevitably combines the data with other more tangible assets and makes isolating the component that covers the data portion almost impossible.

For many categories of oil company data there is no way to replace it, if the past production profile of a well is mislaid there is no way to travel back in time to re-acquire the data. Once a well is completed the original log values cannot be measured again.

So, given that data is not widely traded and the cost to reacquire it is prohibitive, the best remaining way to estimate the value is to look at the benefit it delivers to the organization. So how much value does data deliver to the average oil company? Even this apparently simple question is challenging to address.

Estimates from senior executives

It is important to understand the beliefs that senior executives within oil companies have about the value data brings to their organizations. The normal reason for estimating the value that data delivers is in order to define and present a business case, and the first audience for the business case will be the budget holders, that is, the senior executives. If the proposed intervention does not get approval because the case is not credible the project probably won't go ahead.

There is some evidence for the views of senior managers that is freely available from Common Data Access Limited (CDA) in the UK. They are a membership organization that coordinates the exchange of data between UK oil companies, with participation from the majority of active E&P organizations active in Great Britain.

Figure 2: CDA have published a study of data value in the oil industry[4]

In 2011, they conducted a study in which senior managers were asked to estimate the value that data delivered. The study included input from Norwegian and UK companies active in the North Sea with a few oil companies from other regions such as the Middle East.

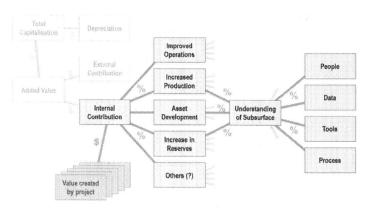

Figure 3: The simplified model used by the CDA study

The study started with a simplified model of how an oil company derives value. It assumes that all value is created by projects

---

[4] "The business value case for data management - a study" written by CDA & Schlumberger was published as a four part report and can be downloaded from the web address shown

delivering defined results. These projects can be classified into different groups, focused on distinct activities such as increasing production or developing assets. Each of these types of activity depends, to some extent, on "understanding the subsurface" and that this is, in turn, achieved by a combination of four components.

■ *Purchase of 50% interest cost £5M*	▪ 20 year drilling program to 2030
■ *Spent £20M over 2 years*	▪ 400M barrels from 20 additional wells
■ *Turned down offer of £100M for our stake*	▪ $34M to drill each well
■ *Value created: (100-5-10)/2 => £42½M per year*	▪ FPSO - $3.4B ($170M / well)
	▪ 20M barrels @ $40/bbl => $800M
	▪ Value created: $696M per year

Figure 4: Calculating the value created by two example projects

Defining the value created by projects requires careful assembly of facts from different groups, for example knowing the amount invested to acquire an interest in a property, documenting the spend on developing the asset and being aware of its current market valuation. This is painstaking but straightforward when applied to a single project, however it just clarifies the value of a single activity. In order to extrapolate this single project value to the whole organization the senior managers must be forced to estimate how many of these types of projects are completed in a given year.

The participating executives were each responsible for different sized groups generating ranges of values. Even the smallest of these groups was responsible for creating almost $100M of value every year.

The Management of Oil Industry

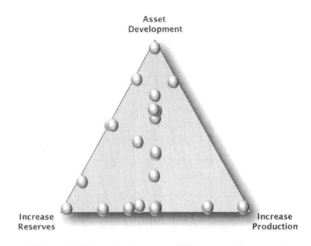

Figure 5: Balancing between different project types

In the CDA study, the participants identified that 95% of the value being created by oil companies came from three different broad categories of projects: increasing reserves; developing assets; or increasing production. The figure above shows how the balance between these three activities varied for all the participating companies.

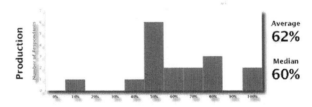

Figure 6: How important subsurface understanding is to production projects

Each of the three main activities has a different dependence on the subsurface. When considering projects that had the aim of increasing production the availability and experience with advanced production technologies has a major impact. In the figure above it can be seen that the most common estimate of the impact of subsurface understanding on production projects was 50%. That is most participants felt that half the success of a production based project came from understanding the reservoir properties.

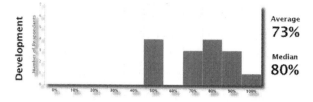

Figure 7: How important subsurface understanding is to development projects

When considering development projects the dependence on the subsurface knowledge was somewhat greater.

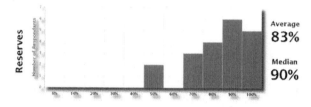

Figure 8: How important subsurface understanding is to reserves projects

Finally, the projects that focused on estimating reserves were naturally seen as having the greatest dependence. The most common estimate was that 90% of the value of these projects came from the subsurface understanding.

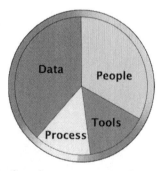

Figure 9: Contribution of components to subsurface understanding

When the senior executives were asked about the components that contributed towards the subsurface understanding, they were universally happy to accept that a combination of people, data, processes and tools were both necessary and sufficient. However, when asked to assign a relative priority to these four elements they were all reluctant to consider them in isolation. After some pressing they did assign relative contributions, the resulting numbers assigned the greatest importance to the data. The sample was limited to senior executives from 22 companies, so while the data component did score more highly than the people, it was not significantly higher. The final result was that data and people were approximately equally important as was the combination of the tools and business processes.

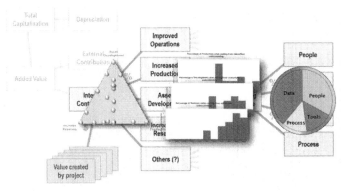

Figure 10: Combining the various components

Each participant described their balance between production, development and reserves, how much each of those activities depended on their understanding of the subsurface and how much data contributed to that understanding. So these factors can easily be combined to deliver an overall estimate of the total value that is created by the data.

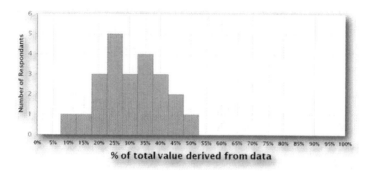

Figure 11: The contribution of data to oil company results

The final result is that each oil company was generating a value of hundreds to thousands of millions of dollars per year, and that between a third and a quarter of that value could be directly associated with the data it held.

If most companies held a single asset that was generating $100M per year in value what would they spend to maintain that asset? How much should they be prepared to invest to increase the value it delivers?

This CDA study demonstrated that, if the beliefs of senior oil company executives are to be trusted, the subsurface data that E&P companies hold is contributing a significant proportion of the overall value created each year.

Estimates from impact statements

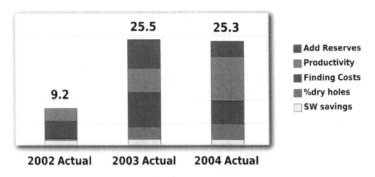

Figure 12: The impact of rationalizing process[5]

There have also been a number of studies that measure the impact of process rationalization. For example, in 2006, one project to reduce the number of applications in Burlington, a North American oil company was justified by the savings in license and maintenance costs (over a three year period). These savings were achieved (shown as "SW savings" in the figure above), however, when the overall improvement was measured later it was found that the simpler data landscape had actually delivered more than 20 times this financial benefit by increasing productivity, reducing the costs of finding data, and other business level effects.

Documenting this type of impact on the business requires input from the users, the management, the financial experts and various domain specialists. This will usually reveal the type of intricate and significant connections that the underlying data has on the total success of an E&P business.

A number of oil companies have conducted internal studies to measure the impact of projects to improve data handling. Burlington was unusual in that they were prepared to present their conclusion in a public forum. It is common to find that improving

---

[5] From "Improving Investment Technology Planning with Metering" by Dan Shearer & Debbie Garcia presented at PNEC 10 – Houston 2006

the information flow delivers benefits that are at least ten times greater than the "obvious" cost saving.

Estimates from models

Another approach that has assisted in documenting the impact of data handling is to model the activities within an oil company.

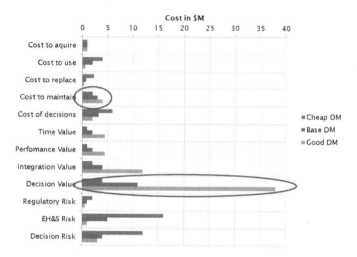

Figure 13: Using a model to estimate the impact of data management[6]

When this was done for Hess in Houston a number of different strategies for data management were tested against the resulting model. The most significant effect was seen to arise from increasing the investment in the maintenance of data. Increasing the amount spent on maintaining data from $3M/year to $4M/year resulted in more than $20M/year extra revenue from the resulting improvement in business decisions.

Of course the exact numbers vary from one oil company to the next, but this type of dramatic improvement in the value of decisions when data quality is improved is also supported by

---

[6] From "Quantitative Value of Data and Data Management" by Paul Haines & Mark Wiseman presented at PNEC 15 – Houston 2011

anecdotal evidence, and is in line with the other results that have already been discussed.

The value of data

So a variety of studies have shown that E&P data is responsible for creating tens to hundreds of millions of dollars value to oil companies. Of course data on its own is not delivering this value, it has to be manipulated by experienced staff and analyzed by reliable tools, but without trustworthy data any oil company would rapidly become a target for being taken over by a rival.

Oil companies invest in their people, for most of them the suggestion that the cheapest possible geoscientists should be hired would be laughable. Selecting tools by price is obviously also a false economy, oil companies take pride in using the most up to date hardware and applications. But, in contrast, most oil companies will focus on how to further reduce their already stretched data management budget. It is as though they think that good data handling is a commodity that could be purchased off the street. At the moment this is certainly not yet true. Profligate spending on data management would be just as short sighted, any company that "threw money at the problem" without careful review would most likely waste it.

The only rational approach is to treat data management as an opportunity for investment, measure the impact that data is having and understand which activities increase or decrease the overall value generated. Where spending more on data handling can be justified by the increase in value, more should be spent. Where cutting costs doesn't negatively impact the results, cut costs.

An army moves at the speed of its slowest soldier. The fact that Wellington was obsessed with ensuring his troopers had good boots was one of the deciding factors in his success in the Peninsula Campaign against the French. The fact that most E&P companies have focused on cutting costs in the past means that at the moment data handling efficiency is frequently the key limiting factor in the effectiveness of an oil company. Investing in this one component can free up other aspects and hence will often deliver a disproportionate benefit.

3. E&P data for the non-specialist

Oil companies are some of the most valuable organizations in the world, participants in the share markets are willing to invest large sums of money to acquire a stake in their future earnings. These investors are taking a bet on future performance based on the company's understanding of resources deep under the surface. For most oil fields there is no way to know the precise shape or future production capacity, there are a number of techniques that deliver some estimates, but these are inherently uncertain and often later turn out to be wrong. Fortunes have been made and lost from different beliefs about the potential that new discoveries could deliver.

 The combination of a very high value, risky interpretations and a wide range of very distinct ways to gain insight has created a number of specialist disciplines, each of which has their own jargon, data, applications, vendors and business processes. The most successful companies have been those that combine the input from these various specialists in innovative ways, companies that rely on repeating past success soon find that more inventive competitors have overtaken their achievements.

Some experienced personnel that have never worked outside the oil industry like to believe that their requirements are extremely specific. It is not unusual to be berated by someone with a grubby boiler suit hanging on the back of their office door who believes that only those who have actually worked on an oil rig are capable of managing the data requirements back in headquarters. This is of course just chauvinism, if it wasn't such a destructive force it would be amusing.

Effective E&P data handling requires a unique combination of skills, knowledge and capabilities. But, there again, effective data handling for banking, retail or aerospace also each require a unique combination of skills, knowledge and capabilities. The techniques that work well for aerospace will not all apply well to financial institutions. From the point of view of data management E&P is just another unique industry.

The first impression of an expert in data management that newly arrives in the oil industry is usually confusion in the face of the bewildering complexity. Often their reaction is to underestimate just how different the views of the various specialists are, it is not uncommon for consultants to suggest that consolidating all the E&P data into a single data model would "simplify the business processes". Of course this has been tried many times before, and never succeeded.

The goal of this chapter is to provide just enough of an outline of the various data categories involved for those new to the oil industry to appreciate how they relate to each other. Hopefully this will give a flavor of how data really functions in a working oil company.

What is data?

Up to this point the term "data" has been used rather loosely. Naturally most geoscientists do not have much formal training in either the theory of computing or semiotics. These subjects seem remote, theoretical and irrelevant to the task of actually generating wealth. This means that domain specialists, when they think of data at all, think of it as either being the raw measurements obtained from the field, or as being "things held in databases".

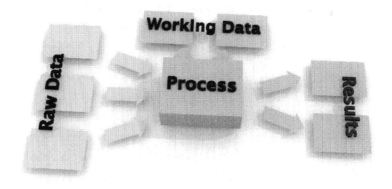

Figure 14: Overly simplified view of the specialist's activities

This view is rooted in the simple picture that each specialist has of their own participation in the overall business process. In this view there is "raw data" that is obtained from "someone else", there is working data that they need to keep track of things and there are results that they deliver to others. If this picture is to be believed then there are two distinct types of data: input data which the specialist requires to do their job; and working data that is their private concern. They see the results they deliver as "knowledge", not data. Under this view the working data may be held in a database of some sort, for example, associated with a particular application.

This simplistic view obscures a number of serious challenges:

- The so called "raw data" is nothing of the sort, usually this information is someone else's results
- When the "working data" really is a temporary work area for the specialist to try out various scenarios it is fair enough for them to have complete control over it. However, usually some parts of this type of data have continued value to the organization for years to come, when the specialists have moved on will their replacements be able to use this data or will they have to start again from scratch?

- Results are data too. Indeed, one would hope that results are data that is significantly more valuable than the inputs used to obtain them (otherwise the effort was not worth it)

Data is available in a number of forms, some of it will, of course, be stored in formal databases, but the majority of data used for business processes won't be. Much of the important data is to be found in spread-sheets, reports and presentations. In the oil industry it is common to have physical documents that hold the definitive version of certain results, for example the officially recognized description of the work carried out on a well is commonly the physical document delivered to the government. This is both because many governments can't cope with modern formats and, more importantly, because the physical document is signed by someone in authority in the oil company who can be tracked down later if something goes wrong.

Sometimes having a physical document is entirely appropriate, for example one company in Egypt that had an interest in a dozen or so wells, but didn't operate any, had their definitive data in a physical file. Everyone knew this was to be found on a particular engineer's desk. If anyone wanted to refer to the data they just copied the appropriate sheets, when information was updated the old sheets were removed and new ones put in their place. This system worked extremely well, having a digital form of the data would have been both harder to manage and more likely to go wrong.

How hard can it be?

Discussing data management with oil industry executives often leads them to ask, "why is managing this data so difficult?" Oil companies typically have a clearly described set of activities, often expressed in the form of a "Value Chain"[7] that progresses assets from exploration, through development to production and finally to abandonment.

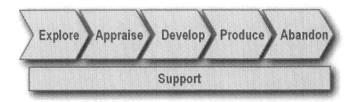

Figure 15: Typical oil company Value Chain

Commonly this set of activities is expressed in terms of a sequence of steps, like that shown above. The hint that this picture is a bit too over simplified is given by the "support" box (often there are a stack of these "generic" activities under the main flow).

It is certainly true that a particular asset will go through a "lifecycle", it will be identified, appraised, developed, produced and abandoned. It is also true that, in many oil companies, there are distinct departments that focus on particular elements of this overall process. But, as the support box hints, there are often other groups that cannot be so neatly pigeon holed.

To give an example, oil companies are commonly organized with distinct departments maybe something like production, exploration, drilling and legal. The role of the production department is to optimize the volumes being produced, so clearly they are focused on the "Produce" step, however they will also play an important role when the field is being developed, scoping the required facilities for example. Also the decision to abandon a field always requires at least the acquiescence of the production group. The exploration department usually has key roles to play in all the first three stages depicted here. The drilling group is

---

[7] Different oil companies use distinct names for this sequence: "asset lifecycle"; "oilfield lifecycle"; and "value chain" are just the three most common variants

potentially involved in all these stages, and the legal group almost certainly are.

This is not intended as a criticism of the "Value Chain". While it is clearly a good way to consider the changing roles of an asset and to focus on the activities and milestones that need attention, this picture, like all simple diagrams, only illuminates one aspect of the overall processes. It is a good model when discussing the maturing of assets, but it is not a useful picture when considering activities with a less focused scope such as personnel, legal management and information handling.

Assembly Line   Blackboard

Figure 16: Different metaphors for data handling in E&P companies

The succession of tasks is implicitly based on an assembly line, where each station understands where it fits in the overall process, what it requires and what it needs to deliver to the next stage. Most information based processes don't match this metaphor very well (either inside or outside the oil industry). A much better one is the "blackboard" where a range of experts start writing what they know, each expert then refines this knowledge, using results from the group and adding more so that the overall group knowledge expands towards fulfilling a goal.

This more generic approach is a more dynamic and flexible way to combine expertise. It allows each expert to contribute when they can and, for complex tasks, its "requirements driven" scheduling makes better use of resources. It has the disadvantage that no single authority controls the complete activity, since no one can be an expert in all of the contributing topics. In the eighteenth century Adam Smith pointed out that for repetitive tasks the assembly line is more efficient, but oil companies rarely make new discoveries doing repetitive tasks.

Figure 17: The activities each interact with data differently

So, given that the blackboard is a better metaphor than the assembly line, what does that tell us about the information flows of a typical oil company? For one thing, the way that users within the organization really share their knowledge is an important consideration. Companies hold databases, spread-sheets, application files and documents that collectively both contain the essential information and are the communication channels through which different disciplines coordinate their efforts to achieve corporate goals.

Understanding which components play these roles, how they are passed from one business activity to another, and how different disciplines view these various repositories is the key to tracking how information works within an oil company.

Main data domains

There are many different groups of technical data that are important to oil companies, and many different ways to classify them. One way is to group data by the departments that utilize it, but this leads to confusion when important elements, such as well headers are claimed by the drilling department, geology, the reservoir engineers and facilities design.

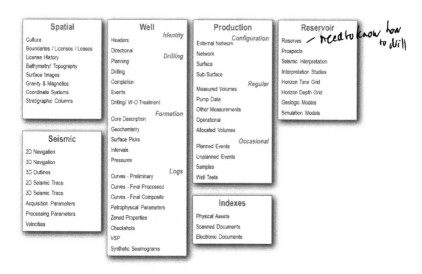

Figure 18: One possible categorization of E&P data

An alternate classification scheme that has been widely applied is to organize data according to its "identifier", so, since well logs are located by first finding the well, they are part of that cluster of data categories. A listing of the key technical data categories using this approach is shown in the diagram above. The critical aspect here is consistency rather than worrying too much about the justifications for placing categories within particular groups. For example, "Velocity Seismic Profiles" (VSPs) which are listed here under logs, can just as validly be listed under seismic, since they measure the speed of sound, or wells, since they are measured down the well bore, or reservoir, since they record features of the field.

Any classification scheme will end up with components that someone will want to debate. The best approach is to compromise, defining a listing that all participants will grudgingly accept, preferably with everyone equally unhappy. The goal here is to understand the intricacies of information flows within a particular organization, rather than to debate the fine details of each and every data category.

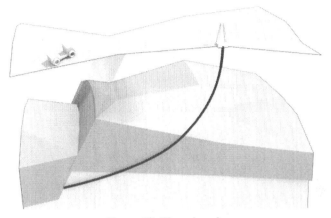

Figure 19: The subsurface

Most of the important technical data is associated with the subsurface, a realm that cannot normally be directly observed. Understanding what is going on in a typical reservoir is like a detective story, various clues are gathered, a theory is put forward, when additional evidence demonstrates that this interpretation was incorrect the theory is refined and new clues are sought. There are many different sources of potentially relevant information.

Drilling

Figure 20: Drilling rig in South Texas[8]

The majority of hydrocarbon resources are obtained by drilling under the surface. This process is complex, expensive and fraught

---

[8] Photograph of the Swanson Drilling Rig One taken 2011 by John Campbell

with risk. Most oil companies have specialized groups, the "Drilling Department" that oversee these operations, even when the actual drilling itself is carried out by external "drilling contractors".

The main activities managed by these groups are:

- **Planning:** Defining the location, equipment and timing of the operations
- **Drilling:** Monitoring and managing the actual boring of the hole
- **Logging:** Measuring the properties of the rocks near the borehole
- **Completion:** Perforating, inserting the casing and other down-hole equipment necessary to efficiently extract oil or gas

The drilling department in most oil companies is typically fairly isolated from the rest of the subsurface groups. They have their own way of working and their own unique suite of applications and data repositories. The use of specialized suites of software that manage drilling data is common, but many drilling departments still heavily rely on Excel spread-sheets and physical documents.

During the planning phase there is a lot of interaction with other groups, the location and path of a well is commonly discussed with the exploration department, legal, reservoir engineering and management. Typically exploration will suggest where a proposed well should go and drilling will explain why such a location is physically impossible, legally undesirable or too risky to be attempted.

While operations are underway, there will often be a daily "morning meeting" to review yesterday's progress and issues. This mainly broadcasts information to the rest of the organization from the drilling group, in many places it is replaced by, or supplemented by a daily email sent to all interested parties.

The Management of Oil Industry

Once a well has been completed it would normally have a "well file" created that describes the key attributes, explains the equipment installed and so on. In many countries there is an obligation to deliver this document to the governing authorities within a specified time period. Because this is closely tied to the contract with the government, the definitive version of this is commonly a physical document that incorporates signatures.

Well measurements

One way to identify subsurface features is to measure properties of rocks that are in contact with or near to the drilled boreholes. There are measurements that are taken directly, for example it is common for "core samples" to be brought to the surface where they can be sent to laboratories for analysis. There are also "outcrops", where particular formations occur at the surface, that are frequently visited by geoscientists. But the most widely employed measurements are those obtained from wire-line logging tools. The logging process lowers a tool through the borehole and measures properties of the subsurface formations.

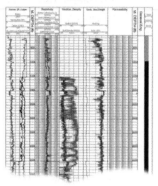

Figure 21: Measurements taken down the borehole[9]

There are a bewildering assortment of different tools, each with their own type of measurement, each with their own special requirements and constraints on how the data can be applied. This work is normally carried out by specialist (known as a petrophysicist) who delivers their results as a set of corrected log curves to the rest of the organization.

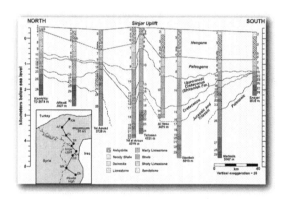

Figure 22: Well correlation panel[10]

Once the petrophysicist has defined the final well logs they can be "picked". This process involves examining the curves from

---

[9] This example and others in this section are courtesy of the U.S. Geological Survey (USGS) from http://www.usgs.gov

[10] This example is from "Tectonic evolution of northeast Syria: Regional implications and hydrocarbon prospects", by G. Brew, R. Litak, M. Barazangi and T. Sawaf, GeoArabia, 4, 389-318, 1999

---

multiple wells in order to identify patterns that indicate important features. For example, one combination of curves might indicate a sandstone and another a shale. Often the particular shapes of different responses allow the expert to identify not just the rock type but where the important formations occur within each well. Combining this understanding with data such as fossil ages (from cuttings) and scanning electron micrographs (SEM) from core samples allows the construction of a cross section that shows the trends of the main formations across an area. Of course this understanding is restricted to just the areas around each wellbore, the features between the wells are too distant to be measured this way.

Seismic

Measurements taken down the well provide an enormous level of detail about the rocks within a few meters of the borehole. Most of the subsurface is, however not that close to a wellbore. Over the years a variety of techniques have been used to generate a wider view, such as measuring variations in gravity or magnetic anomalies. By far the most widely applied of these "geophysical" techniques is seismic.

This employs some source of sound at the surface such as hitting the ground or setting off an explosion, a range of receivers then listen for the echoes as the seismic waves reflect off underground features.

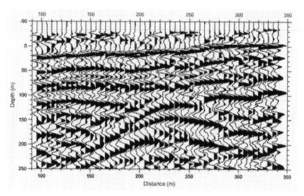

Figure 23: Seismic section[11]

The techniques used to process these raw acoustic waves are complex and difficult to apply. Many oil companies employ specialist "seismic processing" companies to take the original measurements (called "pre-stack" data) and create two or three dimensional arrays that combine multiple measurements into usable seismic volumes. Typically the data will be moved around in specialized formats defined by the Society of Exploration Geophysicists, the so-called SEG formats. The most widely used of these are SEG-D for measured data and SEG-Y for processed seismic.

---

[11] This data is from "SEGY to ASCII Conversion and Plotting Program 2.0" by Mark Goodman courtesy of USGS

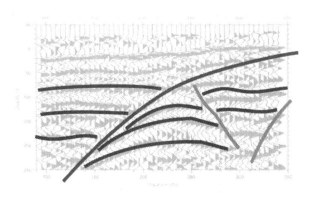

Figure 24: The seismic interpretation identifies surfaces and faults

Once the seismic data has been processed it will typically be "interpreted". Specialized applications allow the geophysicist to identify features such as surfaces and faults. These are combined to provide a model of the area. This seismic based model has two major limitations. Firstly, the vertical scale is set by the speed of seismic waves, rather than by physical depth, that is the vertical scale is in "two way time". Because the speed of sound varies from one rock type to another this distorts the shape. The second limitation is that the typical seismic source has a wavelength of something like 50m, so any subsurface features less than 20m in size cannot be seen.

Geology

As has already been mentioned during the process of interpreting the seismic data the geophysicists start to construct a "model" of the subsurface features. In order to convert this seismic model to depth, and more importantly to distinguish the fine detail of the subsurface these models must be combined with the measurements taken down the borehole.

The interpreter has to identify how the features in the seismic model match up to the picks in the wellbores. The actual location of key points can be worked out from the wellbores, this allows the seismic model to be converted from two way time into depths. By extrapolating the extra detail that can be seen in the wellbores, the model can be filled in with surfaces that are too close for seismic to see them.

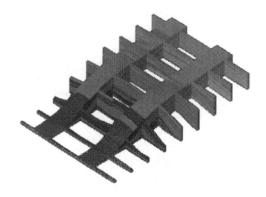

Figure 25: A static model of the subsurface features

These "static models" combine evidence of the large scale elements from the seismic with finer detail from well measurements and analogous components from outcrops and previous work. The difficulty is that there is always a lack of detail so some key aspects of the model come from the experience of the interpreters. When looking for reservoirs of oil or gas the geologists attempt to identify a number of subsurface features, such as source rock, traps and seals.

Reservoir Engineering

Once the structure of a subsurface field has been agreed the next challenge is to work out what will happen if it is disturbed. If a well is drilled what fluids will flow? Would drilling a new well and injecting water be economic?

These questions require a dynamic simulation of the reservoir, one that tracks the fluids and how they flow. The calculations are too time consuming to perform with all the detail of the structural model, so someone has to take the subsurface structure and "up-scale" it to create a simpler model that can be tested against various different production strategies. This "simulation model" is then exercised using specialist software to understand how the field will behave.

Another complication is the ownership of the field, often there will be one oil company that "operates" the field on behalf of a group of partners. These partnerships allow oil companies to share the risks (and rewards) so that a major find will be good news for a number of companies. Distributing the risks of several fields amongst the same collection of oil companies makes it easier to justify the high levels of investment required. When the operator wants to develop the field, for example by drilling a new well, they have to get all the partners to agree to fund it. Also, when revenue is generated the whole group must agree to how it is to be shared out. This in turn means that the partners have to agree right at the start on the software they will use to run these dynamic simulations, so that is often written into the partnership agreement and stays in place, sometimes for decades.

Facilities

Once oil has been discovered the field has to be developed before it can become commercial. This often involves significant civil engineering projects, as production, transportation and processing facilities are constructed. These new structures have to be scaled appropriately; it's no good building a liquefied natural gas (LNG) plant capable of handling 10 million cubic meters of gas per day if the field can only produce a tenth of that, and it's also no good having a field producing 10 times what the plant can handle.

The long lead time for construction means that this is one of the major expenses, the fact that oil companies work in partnerships makes funding easier but makes managing these projects more difficult.

Production

Once a field is commercial it is crucial to keep an eye on the quantities of oil (and gas, and water) it is producing. Not only does this determine the current profit being generated (and passed to partners) but it also provides a check against the various models, so that future revenue can be protected.

The amount of oil produced by a field varies from one year to the next, almost always declining as the fluids are drained. This decline is arrested by intervening in a field, for example by drilling new wells, applying treatment, introducing new technology or changing the way the oil is procured.

Finances

The costly activities of the oil companies, drilling wells, doing work-overs on existing wells, building facilities and so on, are all financially tracked and modeled. For example, the decision to drill one more well in a field will estimate the extra oil that will be produced and contrast that with what will happen if the well is not drilled and this will be balanced against spending the same money in a different region. The long lead time for these activities means that they must take into account things like the price oil will be in 10 years' time.

4. Current practice

Since oil companies are amongst the highest revenue earning organizations on the planet, and the data that they hold is both crucial for their continued profitability and often irreplaceable, one might expect that the data custodians would be the most prestigious, and highly paid, specialists in the industry. This is, however, not the case.

Corporate size & maturity metrics

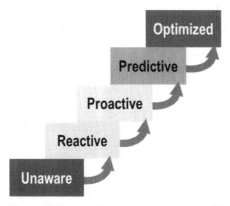

Figure 26: Levels of maturity in data handling

In the 1990s, the "Software Engineering Institute" (SEI) introduced the formal concept of maturity into discussion about the handling of data (and other aspects of computer usage). They suggested that the handling of data can be thought of as having five different levels of maturity:

- **Unaware:** The organization does not recognize that data handling has any significant impact on the corporate performance
- **Reactive:** The organization only invests in improving data handling when there is an issue which becomes unavoidable

---

- **Proactive:** The data managers are able to present a case for improving data management to address anticipated issues
- **Predictive:** The effectiveness of data management is measured and actions can be taken to improve the overall system
- **Optimized:** A continual set of metrics is monitored to ensure the investment in data handling delivers a maximal impact on the business results

Over the succeeding years the way that maturity is assessed has been refined and this measure has been applied to ever finer scales, the original concept continues to prove extremely valuable as a simplified way of contrasting the different approaches used.

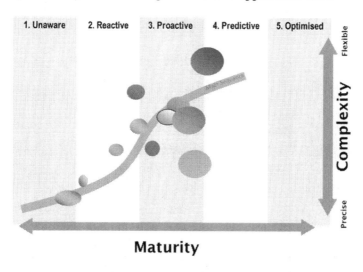

Figure 27: Comparison of maturity against complexity for some oil companies[12]

During the early 2000s, it was noticed that data management maturity has a rough correlation with the complexity of the information landscape within a given company. When the complexity of different oil companies' data environments are

---

[12] Adapted from Kozman, J. "The Main Sequence: Matching Data Management Change to the Organization" (2008) presented at PNEC 12 - Houston

plotted against their maturity the results tend to fall along a "standard sequence". The reasons for this are not hard to imagine, as a company imposes more a more systematic approach they are able to extract extra business value from having a wider range repositories.

One might imagine that within an oil company having as few locations for data as possible would be the best approach. However this is naïve. The reason for having specialists such as petrophysicists, geophysicists and reservoir engineers is that each provides a distinct view, the most successful oil companies are those that best integrate these competing domains. Any oil company that publicly declared it was going to do without, say, reservoir engineers would find its share price rapidly dropping. Each of these specialists has their own way of gathering the evidence they need, integrating and interpreting it and presenting the results so that they can contribute to the company's success.

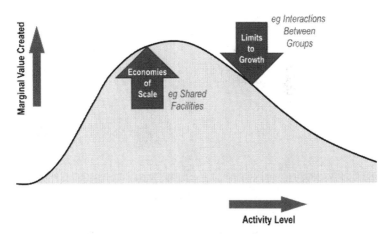

Figure 28: Each data management strategy has an optimal size

For any single approach to data management there are two opposing influences. Economies of scale boost the value generated as more information is handled, while increasing complexity means that a larger operation has limits to the maximum size it can grow to. For small levels of activity it is the economies of scale that dominate, for larger groups the complexity overwhelms the other features.

This is extremely well known in many fields, for example, the way a bird flies means that there is a range of sizes that are appropriate, flying birds cannot be too small, because of the limitations of muscle sizes, or too big, because at larger sizes the proportional strength of bone is not sufficient. When designing something to fly at greater than the speed of sound the dynamics of a bird's wings just won't work, it requires wings that are much stronger and a propulsive unit that is much more powerful.

Just as with flight, there is a way to deal with a larger volume of data, adopt a different strategy. In the case of flight, insects, birds and jet airplanes each employ a distinct way of getting airborne. However, if a graph of their weight and speed is plotted they all fall along a single curve whose shape is dictated by the laws of physics.

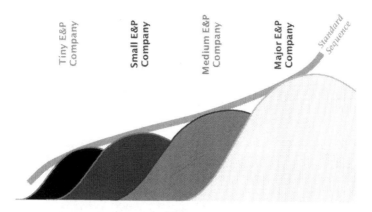

Figure 29: Different strategies match distinct activity levels

In the case of E&P data management, the overall shape of the "standard sequence" is set by the laws of business, but, just like with insects and birds, that does not mean that all organizations adopt the same approach to managing their data. When real companies are examined it has been found that there are four different groups of strategies that are commonly adopted.

Corporate Size	Winning Element	Staff Sizes	Description
Tiny	Property	<20	Focused on one or two assets, tight knit team that all understand their roles and relationships. Little need for formal data management
Small	People	5-200	Focused on a number of assets. Finding the data is a matter of knowing who to ask
Medium	Portfolio	50-2000	Balancing risks across a range of assets. Key data is managed in set locations within the asset, some assets do this well.
Major	Process	>500	Staff are mobile between assets. Key data is managed corporately, all data is managed in set locations. Focus is on defining and enforcing the "corporate way" of doing things

Figure 30: Different sized oil companies need different strategies

Tiny E&P companies will achieve significant success if the property they own becomes valuable. Small companies rely on having the best people in key positions, a single success will only sustain them for a limited period but a star asset manager might deliver above average results for many years. Medium companies have too many staff for them all to be rising stars, they achieve success by balancing out high-risk, high pay-out assets against a steady stream of low risk, low pay-out ones. Major companies have to continue to wring the maximum value from their portfolios but, in addition, attempt to out-compete their rivals by ensuring that their internal processes are as efficient as possible.

The optimal data management strategy for a particular E&P company depends on which of these categories it is in, or plans to be in. Defining procedures for every eventuality makes sense when there is a rapid turn-over of staff and the cost can be spread across many countries. In a 12 man company this attention to detail would be crippling.

The impact of software purchasing

Since the 1980s, the expansion of procurement departments with aggressive cost reduction targets has forced software vendors to hide purchasing costs in less easily monitored forms. This type of dynamic is fairly common in other industries, printer manufacturers realized they could get a larger margin from consumables than from the initial purchase and started subsidizing printers, games console vendors sell hardware at less than the cost of its components confident that the extra margin on the software will more than make up for it.

In the E&P software world this dynamic has made selling software that "integrated" data across a range of disciplines a challenging task. The purchasing processes within oil companies has traditionally been configured to pay the minimum amount it could for software to support a focused, tightly defined, set of activities. Any vendor that incorporated tools to consolidate the wide range of inputs that were required for real work finds itself undercut by a competitor that refused to deliver anything that wasn't explicitly specified in the original purchase request.

The determination of major oil companies to pay the minimum price for software has limited the profitability that independent software developers can realize, making them vulnerable to being taken over by one of the few major vendors whose size and diversity gives them the leverage to realize the necessary revenue. It is not clear that this result is in the oil companies' best interests.

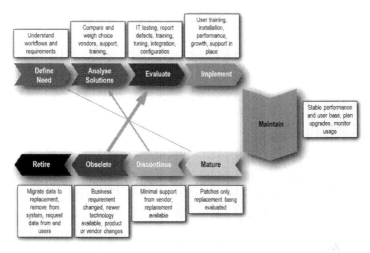

Figure 31: Application deployment lifecycle within an oil company[13]

Most oil companies have defined processes for identifying, evaluating and implementing new applications. When users perceive that a new innovation will make their tasks easier there is a fairly widely understood process that must be followed to bring new software into the organization. Often a single vocal proponent will be sufficient. In contrast, the task of identifying the applications that are now obsolete is more challenging. It usually takes a long time for every single user to switch to alternative software, and as long as there is still at least one user gaining value from an older suite of applications there is a natural bias to hold on to the familiar tools.

This reality means that many oil companies have a large number of applications that are each used by a few specialists. Each of these will typically have their own private store of data and its own specialized links to the rest of the company's systems. This encourages the "information landscape" within a company to grow in complexity.

---

[13] Adapted from "Improving technology investment planning with metering" by Dan Shearer & Debbie Garcia - PNEC 2006

Method Standards

There are many different standards used within the industry to control activities. These have their origins in generic cross-industry attempts to impose systematic controls on complex business processes.

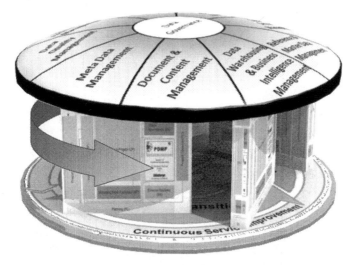

Figure 32: The data management roundabout[14]

The three most important standards for data handling are the Data Management Body of Knowledge (DMBoK), the project management standards and the Information Technology Infrastructure Library (ITIL). These are complementary to each other. One expert suggested that they can be thought of as three levels of an ever rotating roundabout, ITIL defines the underlying on-going services, improvements are implemented within projects and these are all under the umbrella of DMBoK which coordinates the programme to work towards a consistent vision.

---

[14] Based on an original idea from Nigel Corbin in "Information Requirement" presented at ECIM 2010

Data Management

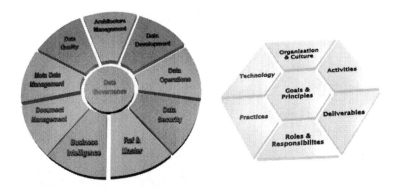

Figure 33: DMBoK explores 10 functions by reviewing the 7 elements

The most widespread data management methodology is that described by a group called Data Management International (DAMA) within their "Data management Body of Knowledge". Since this is such an important technique it will be covered in the next chapter – "The Data Management Body of Knowledge".

Projects

There are a number of different project management standards that have been adopted within the oil industry, the most widely used of which are PRINCE2[15] and PMI[16]. The goals of these two methodologies are fairly similar, imposing a structured approach to the activity of project management. Both methodologies emphasize the "business case" for the project, ensuring that this is written down and available to all participants.

---

[15] PRojects IN Controlled Environments 2 (PRINCE2) was developed by the UK government as the project management standard for public projects and is now established as a standard approach for project management in many industries
[16] The Project Management Institute (PMI) is a US based professional organization for the project managers. They have published the "Project Management Body of Knowledge" (PMBoK)

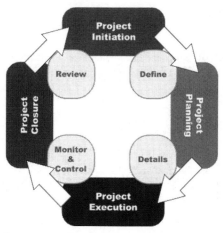

Figure 34: PMI divides projects into processes

Both PMI and PRINCE2 are also very clear on the management reporting roles, in particular focusing on "management by exception". That is, on the project manager being given a target and "tolerance" and seeking guidance as soon as it becomes apparent that these constraints won't be met. For example, if phase one should be completed by the end of January, with a tolerance of one month, then the project manager can take whatever actions they feel are necessary as long as they anticipate completion before the end of February. However, as soon as they suspect that this date will be exceeded they must report this to the "board", propose a change to the project and seek permission to execute it. These tolerances can be set on timeframes, spend, resources used, project goals or anything else that the project board feels need to be controlled.

For data management to be effective the particular project management methodology employed is not overly important. On the other hand it is crucial that a systematic approach to projects is taken, and that the business goals of projects are discussed and documented. PMI, PRINCE2 and many other project management methodologies clearly define the things that are necessary, any of them can be used effectively as part of a reasonable data management approach.

The Management of Oil Industry

Services

The management of services is quite distinct from project management. Good projects all have a defined business goal and an anticipated completion date. Services, in contrast, are often expected to carry on as long as the customer has a need that the supplier is willing to fulfill.

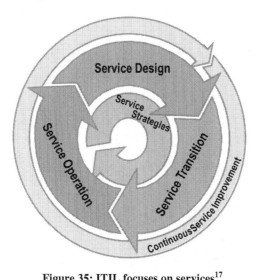

Figure 35: ITIL focuses on services[17]

The Information Technology Infrastructure Library (ITIL) is a collection of practices for the effective delivery of services. The standard is split into five books covering: Service Strategy; Design; Transition; Operation; and Improvement.

This material provides formal definitions for terms that have been around for some time, such as "Service Level Agreement" (SLA), the "Service Catalogue", "Demand Management" and "Change Management". This material is particularly important for defining the "Data Operations" and, also, for clarifying the roles within the Data Management group.

---

[17] The Information Technology Infrastructure Library (ITIL), is a set of practices for IT service management published by the UK Office of Government Commerce (OGC)

5. The Data Management Body of Knowledge

Data Management International[18] (DAMA) is an independent association of technical and business professionals dedicated to advancing the concepts and practices of information handling throughout the business world. Globally there are more than 50 regionally based DAMA chapters. DAMA have created a number of resources for the data management professional including training courses and international conferences. During 2009 DAMA published the first version of their "Data Management Body of Knowledge"[19] (DMBoK). This extensive standard is being widely adopted in many industries as a framework for performing data management.

Figure 36: DAMA's ten data management functions

The DMBoK divides data management into 10 functions as shown above. Each of these is then described by expanding on 7

---

[18] The DAMA web site at http://www.dama.org/ holds an excellent collection of resources for data managers from all industries
[19] The first edition DMBoK was published as ISBN 978-0977140084

"elements": Goals & Principles; Organization & Culture; Activities; Deliverables; Roles & Responsibilities; Practices & Techniques; and Technology. This framework ensures that this complex topic is explored systematically and in a way that simplifies understanding.

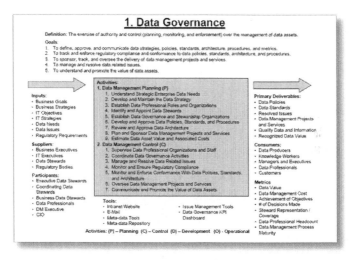

Figure 37: The overview of Data Governance from DMBoK

Here, for example, is the overview of the topic of Data Governance that outlines the key elements of this activity according to DMBoK. The DAMA material provides valuable insights into implementing information management, but there are some areas where E&P industry norms differ from the generic approach that is assumed.

Application to E&P

The DAMA standard was defined by experts from a variety of business sectors and has a goal to be applicable across a wide range of industries. It is hardly surprising that, as one oil industry reviewer rightly commented[20], the standard was "too abstract and offers too little in the way of concrete examples".

---

[20] Neil McNaughton in OilIT - July 2010 (http://www.oilit.com/)

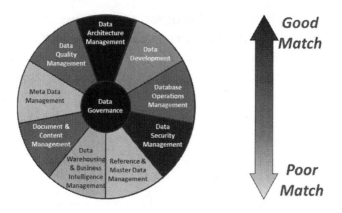

Figure 38: How well the DAMA function descriptions match to E&P data[21]

Most of the DAMA functions are directly applicable to the handling of E&P data and this will be more fully explored in the next few chapters. However there are four areas where the naïve application of the generic DAMA functions would not be effective:

- **Reference & Master Data:** The approach described in DMBoK is exactly the same as has been tried in E&P many times before, most notably in the attempt by the Petrotechnical Open Software Corporation (POSC) to implement Epicentre in the early 1990s
- **Data Warehousing:** The range of technical data has very few commonly agreed attributes, this makes the creation of effective cross discipline data warehouses expensive, up to now this approach has not proved an effective tactic in E&P
- **Physical Data Management:** In the oil industry there is an emphasis on the need to manage physical assets such as core samples. In many other industries this can be considered as part of document management, the oil industry is different

---

[21] From Hawtin, S. "Applying DAMA to E&P Data" originally presented in 2010 at PNEC 14 in Houston

- **Meta Data Management:** The te[r]
  has a number of conflicting meanings
  world, the issues described in DM[B]
  applicable in E&P but less confusion is caus[...]
  this function is renamed "Audit Data Management[...]

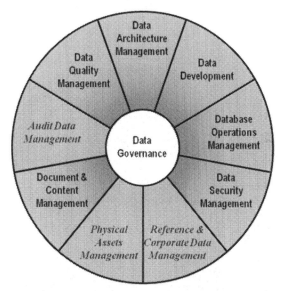

Figure 39: An E&P specialized variant of the DAMA functions

Given the four issues faced above it is more useful to apply the "E&P variant" of the DAMA functions that is shown above. The next few chapters will expand each of these functions in turn focusing on their implementation for subsurface data handling.

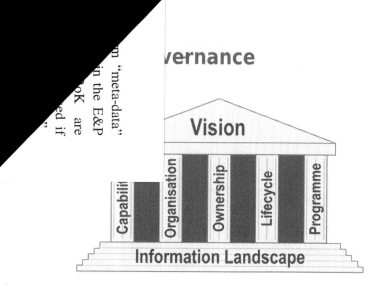

Figure 40: The key aspects of data governance

According to the DMBoK, Data Governance is the "high level control over planning and execution of data management". This description can be a daunting one, especially for those that have never been involved in the setting of corporate strategy before. The main deliverables are shown in the figure above, this checklist of topics focuses on the end results rather than organizing the tasks required to achieve them.

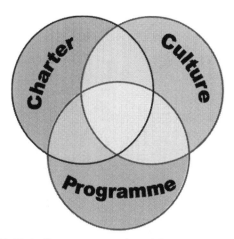

Figure 41: Data Governance consists of three overlapping areas

The alternate view shown above splits the topic into three overlapping areas:

- **Charter:** Documenting the goals of data management, the underlying principles that need to be addressed
- **Culture:** Defining how the management of data interacts with the various communities within the organization
- **Programme:** Controlling the portfolio of projects that are needed to transform the current situation into an improved one

By addressing these three areas, in the order above, a reasonable plan can be assembled to tackle even the most challenging data governance issues.

The data governance charter

The "charter" clarifies the authority and justification for governance. It starts from the underlying principles that can be widely agreed and builds to a set of implementable standards. The level of formality will vary from one organization to the next, some companies will implicitly share a common view of which aspects should be constrained and which left flexible. In larger organizations it quickly becomes apparent that there are widely differing views and that a more formal statement of requirements is needed.

The unwritten elements

It is rare for any organization, even the largest, to explicitly document every single element of the charter. It is much more common to leave at least part of the company "rules to live by" unwritten.

Assumptions of professionalism would imply that <u>all</u> technical users should be conscientious about understanding the limits implied by the data they employ. They should carefully structure their own data, reasonably describe results that they pass to others and extensively document their projects so the data can be reused later. Unfortunately pressures of time and resources mean that anyone maintaining these high standards would be a notable exception rather than the rule.

In smaller organizations, an inability to keep your own data in order, a tendency to pass the wrong results on, or a penchant for leaving projects in a mess will damage both your reputation and your own personal financial prospects. In larger organizations, this type of sloppy approach to data can be obscured by scoring a few notable successes or by repeatedly moving on before anyone notices. For this reason, the various components that make up the charter are written down explicitly more often in larger oil companies where staff move frequently between locations and asset teams.

Vision

One of the most powerful elements to have explicitly documented is the "vision" for data handling in the organization. Ideally, this is a concise and precise description of how everyone is expected to behave when handling data, preferably it will have been endorsed by the highest level of management and incorporated into mandatory training. The need to be comprehensive, universal and short makes this a very difficult document to write, it often employs words such as "ownership", "corporate" or even "data" with very specific, and quite technical, meanings.

#	Vision
1	All data is a strategic asset, whether corporate, shared or isolated and underpins the business decisions of the company
2	All data will be handled in accordance with applicable laws and regulations or company standards, whichever are the more stringent
3	Each professional is responsible for disclosing the quality and uncertainty of the data they share with others and for understanding the limitations of the data they employ
4	The ownership of all shared information should be clearly defined, understood and implemented
5	The creation, use and destruction of corporate data should be carried out in compliance with group standards and legislation
6	Within the constraints of safety, budget and corporate standards the company will take every action to realise the full potential value of data assets
7	Any restriction that data handling standards place on the flexibility of working or the creativity of the company's professionals will be justified by a business case

Figure 42: Example corporate data vision statements

Here is an example of the types of statements that would typically make up a corporate data handling vision. The process of honing these statements requires participation from data users, asset managers and senior executives, usually coordinated by data management experts.

Finally it is, of course, not sufficient to just publish the vision, it must also be adopted. This will usually require some kind of focused change management activity and to be effective some of the elements have to be measured and reported. Often this is best achieved by defining related metrics that are explicitly included in the annual appraisals of middle ranking managers.

Mission

At a less strategic level than the vision come the "data mission" statements. These are usually defined for specific groups within the organization, for example the petrophysicists might all have an aspiration to publish a complete suite of curves for each well analyzed.

Standards

In order to ensure consistency across different groups there are often collections of standards that define the minimal quality required for data before it should be employed. Different organizations each have their own way of classifying standards. The most well thought out schemes employ comprehensive definitions of data categories, locations, business activities, data handling workflows and repositories so that not only is it easier for users to identify applicable documents but, more importantly, it is also possible to list the standards that have not been created yet.

The applicability of standards also has a significant effect. Where the "company standards" are mandatory and compliance is measured they will usually be more comprehensive and widely referred to. In companies where the "data management group" creates standards that the geoscience users can treat as optional or advisory, they will be generally ignored and are often less mature.

Data Ownership

There is one group of standards that is crucial to successful data handling, that is the definition of all the aspects of "data ownership". The concept of data ownership is widely discussed but rarely made explicit. There are many different ideas that are commonly applied.

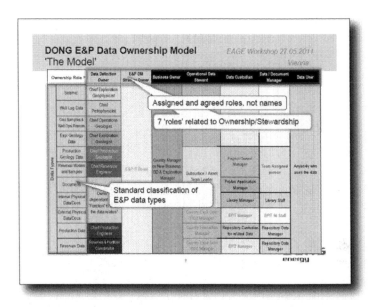

Figure 43: Data Ownership roles adopted within DONG[22]

One notable exception to the general lack of precision in this topic is DONG, the Danish oil company, they have seven different elements of data ownership that they identified:

- **Data Definition Owner:** ensures that a clear definition of the storage mechanisms, reference values and structures is shared by all users
- **DM Strategy Owner:** defines and enforces overall data management strategy
- **Business Owner:** accountable for the quality of data within their asset (also referred to as the Asset Data Manager within this document)
- **Operational Data Steward:** the custodians of data within the asset
- **Data Custodian:** the keepers of corporate data, responsible for ensuring the data is kept exactly as it was submitted (mistakes and all)

---

[22] This is from "DONG E&P - Data Ownership Model" by Kenneth Nordstrøm & Guttorm Vigeland presented at EAGE Workshop Vienna 2011

- **Data / Document Manager:** the owner of documents and other unstructured data
- **Data User:** the users of data, responsible for tracking data quality

Each of these roles has been assigned to a specific group for each identified cluster of data categories (the seismic data, the well logs and so on). This might seem like an over complex list and it may be tempting to imagine that these roles are not distinct in a smaller organization, however experience has shown that this belief is often mistaken. All seven of these roles should normally be identified, even if in some profiles they are assigned to the same individuals.

Defining terms

Even the most knowledgeable practitioner cannot hope to understand all the nuances of handling data across the whole range of E&P domains. In order to make sense of all the workflows, repositories and data categories it is essential to impose some order, that is to define some common concepts and terms that will be applied across the organization.

All the most successful data governance initiatives are grounded in this type of abstract understanding. The main elements that should be included will be discussed later in chapter 7 – "Data Management Architecture".

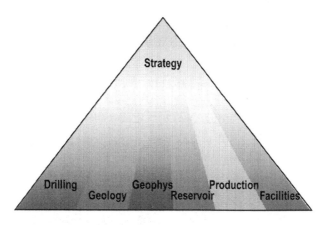

Figure 44: Different domains share an underlying strategy

In general it is worth pointing out that while the specific tasks associated with handling each group of E&P data are very different from each other, at the strategic level all these distinct activities share common elements. By first defining the standards at this more abstract level the individual domains become easier to contrast and compare.

If a simplified model of the activities that are to be included is available then it makes communication between the stakeholders easier. Explicitly writing down the elements of this model makes it more likely that abstract terms such as "Publish" or "Corporate Data" or even "Stratigraphic Column" will not be misunderstood. This is not a simple exercise, a loosely defined term or logical inconsistency can cause no end of confusion.

Documented Principles

The most detailed level of the charter would be a complete listing of the "principles" believed by all the participants. At this time it is believed that no oil company has managed to document such a list.

This would describe all the principles that are accepted across an organization. For example these could be:

- Having a consistent and documented data strategy helps reduce misapplication of data
- Data is only valuable for the duration of the project
- Higher quality data delivers lower risks
- Reducing data handling costs is important
- The cost of acquiring data is more important than the cost of keeping it
- Interpreted data is the private concern of the specialist that creates it
- All the data that contributes to any business decision belongs to the organization

As can be seen from the list above it is not unusual for these principles to directly contradict each other. The majority of oil company staff don't spend their time worrying about data, they have other things to concern them.

This means that a key part of data governance is comprehending the implicitly held beliefs held within the organization and, where they conflict with best practice, identify the training and tools that will educate the users to a better understanding. The most effective approach is to apply the techniques of "change management" to address these issues, a topic that will be touched on in chapter 8.

Culture

Another important aspect of effective data management is the culture of the data users. Frequently, the most challenging aspects of implementing an improvement in data handling are tied to modifying the behavior of individuals rather than improving the tools they employ. In order to clarify the roles that are played by staff in data handling it is important to first understand the way that most oil companies are organized.

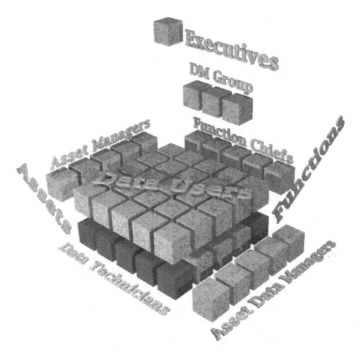

Figure 45: The "normal" structure of an oil company

The main groups are shown in this picture. The data users are normally team members within a particular asset, in addition they have a recognized function and communicate with their opposite numbers working in the same domain for different assets. It is common for the assets to have some kind of "data technicians" who load and manage the data, often these are a mix of company staff and external contractors. The "asset data manager" is responsible for the data handling across the whole asset and reports issues to the asset manager.

At the same time there will be a group of function experts, called something like "function chiefs" or "domain advisors" that define, promote and enforce the corporate wide policies for each functional specialism. In the best companies all these activities are coordinated by a data management group that report directly to the corporate executives.

These many different groups have different levels of participation with data. Some, like the executives, just need to be kept informed while others, like the asset data managers, should ideally take a far more active role.

In the most effective companies, all these groups share a consistent vision of how data management should be conducted, have an understanding of the way their current processes match up to this ambition and are committed to moving towards this goal (within the constraints of existing budget). The previous section outlined how this "charter for data" can be documented.

Corporate Control

Obtaining active commitment from senior executives is the most crucial step towards improving data management. They allocate the budget, endorse the vision, set the corporate goals and encourage compliance.

Of course, the most senior executives never get involved in the day-to-day aspects of data handling, but it is essential that they are kept aware of the real impact that data handling is having on their wider business. Without a reasonable understanding of the relative importance they will not be able to balance the budget and justify the costs and efforts needed to optimize the overall performance.

Function Chiefs

Usually there are a group of senior technical specialists that each dictate the way their particular discipline is carried out. For example, often there will be a "Chief Geologist" who documents geological standards and reviews key projects.

The most important way that this group interacts with the data handling is through the data definition standards. The senior users must at least endorse any standards and preferably be involved in the writing, dissemination and enforcement of them.

Asset managers

In most oil companies the asset managers are responsible for the profitability of their asset. Typically asset managers will have a geoscience, operations or finance background; they will usually see data management as "someone else's problem".

Good asset data managers will be able to keep their asset managers aware of the main issues that currently limit performance within their group.

Asset Data Managers

The task of the asset data manager is to understand the impact that current data handling is having on the effectiveness of an asset and to report that to the asset manager.

It is fairly common for this role to be filled by an external contractor, this is seen as being a good way to bring in expertise that the company does not possess. Unfortunately this approach reinforces the impression that data management can be fixed by hiring someone else to do it. The best asset data managers will combine an understanding of all the key data categories with an appreciation for the theoretical and practical limitations of real information systems.

Data users

The various geologists, reservoir engineers, facilities designers, drilling engineers, petrophysicists, geophysicists and production analysts all rely on data to perform their day to day tasks. Usually none of these specialists has any formal training in data handling.

As professionals the responsibility of these users should be quite clear, they should ensure that they understand the data they employ, at least to the level of knowing how much it can be trusted. In addition, they should document any results they send to others to allow the recipient to assess how much they should be able to rely on it. Unfortunately the constraints of time mean that this high standard is almost never achieved, the assumptions made are rarely written down, results are passed on without any attempt to document their precision and they are labeled with ambiguous names that are commonly misunderstood by the recipients.

There is a debate as to whether this flexibility in communicating between disciplines causes any lasting damage. Users usually assert that missteps, where the receiver of data applies it in a way that conflicts with the assumptions the sender made, tend to cancel out, and the overall process is able to come to valid conclusions despite these challenges. Unfortunately this complacent attitude has, in the past, resulted in some significant consequences.

Data technicians

Data technicians, or technical assistants as they are frequently referred to, help the users to handle their data. It used to be that the technical details of loading and extracting information from specialist tools were so detailed and intricate that only an expert could perform the task. Twenty years ago it was common for inexperienced geoscientists to become technical assistants, with the hope that eventually this would lead to a "real" job. However the growing sophistication of software tools, wider familiarity with data loading and the radical squeeze on employing support staff that resulted from the drop in oil price around the year 2000, made good data technicians rare.

A number of oil companies have subsequently realized that their drive to outsource non-core business left them unable to even assess how good a job their data management contractors were doing. As a result in recent years there has been the re-emergence of an information management career path. In many oil companies this in turn has led to an increase in the opportunities available for reliable technical assistants.

Normally data technicians have to satisfy the requirements of three distinct groups, the data users want all data to be "handled" without requiring their involvement, the asset data managers who want every transaction to be clearly documented and the data management group that want to ensure all standards are followed. There are a number of different ways to balance between these three sets of drivers:

- Sometimes organizations ensure that all data technicians are contractors and attempt to manage their objectives through enforcing a formal contract
- Usually data technicians are embedded within the assets, so their proximity to the data users ensures a continued focus on delivering value to the users
- Often the data technicians will have an additional "dotted line", so they report functionally to the data management group, this ensures that annual reviews incorporate measures of how well they have supported corporate standards
- Where data technicians are part of the data management group they are often lent to assets to perform specific activities. This "project based" approach often focuses on goals that the data users don't value highly
- Sometimes data technicians are considered to be part of the IT organization, this is usually down to historical accident rather than conscious design

Whichever combination of these approaches is adopted, it is almost universal that the data technicians focus is on handling the "raw data", that is, information that has been obtained from external contractors and is closer to actual measurements than interpreted results. This bias has a number of deleterious effects, not only does it encourage data users to perpetuate a misleading view of the data flows, it also reinforces a view that the correct loading of data is a "low-value" activity that can be left to the cheapest resource, and it encourages users to treat finalized models and other "results" as their own private concern rather than data of value to the organization.

The Data Management Group

There will often be a group that coordinate the data handling activities across a company. They will usually set standards, coordinate data improvement projects, oversee the activities of the data technicians and asset data managers, and advise the executives on data management matters. Usually the data management group would not directly load data but would be responsible for defining standards for how it is to be loaded.

In smaller companies this group may consist of one or two individuals with a "vision" of how the information should be managed who meet occasionally. As the organization expands the need to enforce a consistent approach to data becomes more and more apparent. In some organizations this group will be part of the IT function, however the most successful approach is to ensure that the data management group has its own, clearly defined, identity.

The structure of the group will obviously depend on what is appropriate for the organization and the role they are to play. It is important to realize that the main role of the data management group is normally to provide a service to the rest of the community, as such the model to follow is that defined in ITIL. This standard includes a comprehensive list of potential roles, and it is useful as a checklist to ensure all key activities are covered. The most obviously applicable roles are:

- **Business Relationship Manager:** maintains a positive relationship with all data users
- **Availability Manager:** defines, analyses, plans, measures and improves all aspects of the availability of services
- **Capacity Manager:** ensures that the agreed capacity and performance targets can be delivered in a cost effective and timely manner
- **Compliance Manager:** ensures that standards and guidelines are followed

- **Enterprise Architect:** maintains a description of the essential components of a business, including their interrelationships
- **Risk Manager:** identifies, assesses and controls risks
- **Service Catalogue Manager:** maintains the service catalogue, ensuring all descriptions are accurate and up to date
- **Service Level Manager:** negotiates Service Level Agreements and ensures that these are met
- **Service Owner:** responsible for delivering a particular service within the agreed service levels
- **Supplier Manager:** ensures that value for money is obtained from all suppliers
- **Change Manager:** controls the lifecycle of all changes
- **Configuration Manager:** maintains information about the configuration items required
- **Knowledge Manager:** ensures that information about these services is gathered, stored and shared across the organization
- **Project Manager:** plans and coordinates the resources to deliver particular projects
- **Incident Manager:** implements the incident management and associated reporting
- **Operations Manager:** ensures the day-to-day operational activities are carried out
- **Service Request Fulfillment Group:** deliver specialized services
- **CSI Manager:** Continual Service Improvement (CSI) Manager is responsible for managing improvements

While even the largest oil companies would not usually have an individual dedicated to each of these roles, the descriptions are a useful checklist to help clarify the responsibilities of each member of the group.

The Programme

There are always more potential projects than can be undertaken within the constraints of funding and available staff. Selecting the best combination to actually implement requires careful balancing of a number of factors. These include the costs and benefits, the fit to corporate objectives, the resources required and the inter-project dependencies.

Figure 46: Projects, services, programmes and strategies

The best organized projects are often grouped together into "programmes". The OGC[23] specifies that a programme must meet a strategic need, must have high level leadership and direction, and must involve a range of activities that combine together to deliver the outcome. They say that programmes often emerge from a growing requirement to encourage cohesion, enforce compliance against a building body of standards and end up being driven by a shared vision.

---

[23] OGC here refers to the "Office of Government Commerce" in the UK. This is the body responsible for the original definition of the PRINCE project management methodology and the ITIL service definition standards. Their "Managing Successful Programmes Manual" defines how to handle groups of related projects.

The distributed financial structure of many oil companies can complicate the adoption of new systems that span organizational boundaries. The additional steps required to overcome these issues should be incorporated within the change management process.

Creating a formal or informal group that coordinates the range of projects will usually ensure a more considered approach is taken; will simplify the process of allocating budget; and will reduce the inefficiency of parallel conflicting projects. For smaller organizations this can be as simple as a regularly held review meeting, larger organizations will find that the wide impact of these projects requires a larger and more formal forum.

Figure 47: The IM programme addresses a range of conflicting requirements

Each information management improvement project can be characterized by its: financial cost; potential financial impact; fit with corporate goals; timing requirements; resource needs; dependencies on other projects; data domain being addressed; assets that will be affected; staff training requirements; business processes; and legal implications. Estimating the impact of each project within a consistent framework will help ensure a balanced set of projects is selected.

Business Case

The financial cost and benefits of projects should always be articulated as part of the essential work to develop a consistent business case. Ensuring that these calculations are performed in a consistent way allows the results to be compared, for example, if two projects assume different internal rates of return this should be justified by their relative risks.

Benefits

Project	Benefit Type A	B	C	D	E	Total
1			20			20
2	5		5	10		20
3	5		5			10
4			20		20	40
5		10		5		15
6		5	5	5	5	20
7	10					10
8		20	20	10		50
Total	20	35	75	30	25	185

Key:
A – customer satisfaction
B – cycle time reduction
C – data quality improvement
D – process improvement
E – decision quality improvement

Figure 48: Different types of benefit have to be considered

The financial return is usually not the only benefit that emerges from a project. For example, one project might improve data quality and so have a pull-through benefit in the anticipated success of later activities. Contrasting the range of benefits that different projects are expected to deliver might lead to the selection of a project that addresses a particular need, even when other candidates have a better financial return.

Corporate Goals

One area of benefits that often gets particular attention is the degree to which each improvement project enables the "corporate goals". In a company where the annual report expresses an aspiration to expand production a project that improves the handling of well intervention plans might be expected to gain additional support. In contrast, if the organization's goal is to ensure full employment in a particular country then a project to reduce the number of technical assistants might be expected to face resistance.

Resources

Each project will require a combination of resources. It is not unusual to discover that two apparently complementary projects cannot proceed in parallel because a particular expert is required to be fully dedicated to both of them.

There is also the impact that projects will have on the users. If users are required to participate then this will disrupt their normal operations. Planning major changes to avoid particularly busy periods will often contribute towards a successful delivery.

Dependencies

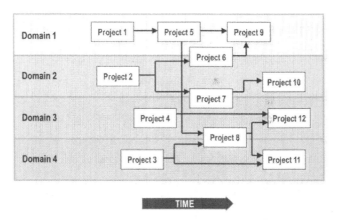

Figure 49: Scheduling dependencies may constrain project start dates

Another element of the programme planning will come from an appreciation of the inter-project dependencies. Often one project cannot be started until another is complete, or there may be benefit in synchronizing two projects in order to ensure the users only have to significantly change their practices once.

7. Data Management Architecture

It has already been claimed that the flows of data within an oil company are a challenge to understand and have unexpected implications for success. One of the most important tasks of any data manager is explaining some of these interactions in ways that engage people many of whom are not obsessed with the details and have other jobs to do.

There is a tendency in bureaucracies to label even the most menial job with a high power name, for example the rubbish collector becomes a "recycling advisory operative", so one might be tempted to think that calling the person that draws data flow diagrams an "architect" is just part of the same tendency. What makes this "architecture"?

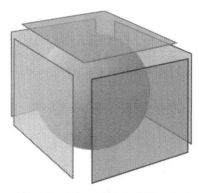

Figure 50: The architect has to coordinate different views for specialists

One way to think about the word is to focus on the multiple specialists that the architect directs. When constructing a building an architect needs to: explain the vision to the client; ensure the planning authorities give approval; check that the necessary utilities are available; tell the building contractor where to dig foundations and construct walls; verify the supplier's' schedules; and direct the electricians and plumbers connecting the internal fixtures. Each of these interactions require communication that focuses on a specialized part of the overall process, it is the architect that ensures the electrician's wiring diagram is consistent with where the walls have been placed.

The thing that makes someone an architect in this view is the fact that they have to appreciate the whole solution, providing a range of distinct pictures that each give just enough context for a particular specialist to work without overwhelming them with unnecessary detail. The architect has to ensure that all the contributors are coordinated and driving towards a common result.

Achieving this requires that a selection of "models" of the company be created. These can then be rendered into simplified pictures that can all be used to inform decisions about future actions. The concept of modeling aspects of corporate activity is central to architecture. One could picture this as a single consistent model in the mind of the architect that is being rendered in a range of specialized views. Alternately, one could envisage that a range of simple models each tailored to a particular purpose are being kept consistent with each other. These two views are, of course, equivalent.

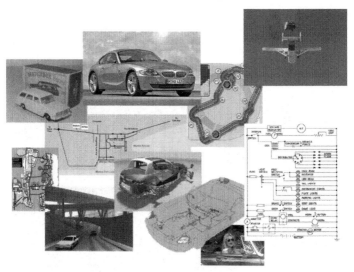

Figure 51: The "best" model is determined by its intended use

It is an obvious statement but worth keeping in mind that the best model of anything is dictated by its anticipated use, not by the thing being modeled. When modeling a car: its weight, acceleration and turning circle need to be understood if the aim is to understand how fast it will go round a track; its color, shape and size if you want to show a physical model in a display case; and if you are creating a picture that a mechanic can use to fix the electrics then a schematic diagram is probably going to be the best "model".

The data management architect is faced with the same type of challenge. They must: document the way data flows at the moment; explain the business benefits that will emerge when some modifications are made; clarify the long term vision of how data should flow; describe the standards that data technicians should adhere to; and educate the users as to why they should invest the time to keep their data in order.

In order to understand an existing situation and propose a potential way it could be improved there must be a set of renditions that capture the essential components and present them in a usable way. These need to be tailored for the audience they are aimed at.

Enterprise Architecture

In other industries it is common to think of data elements as "belonging" to particular data stores or their associated applications. This means that a typical organization can be thought of as having four layers, the infrastructure, the data, the applications and the business processes. The business activities are carried out by manipulating applications that are, in turn, responsible for particular data items.

In E&P this relationship between applications and data is better thought of as being the other way round. There are data items, for example the representation of a well, that exist within multiple, incompatible applications. So in this case, the applications and their associated repositories, act as a temporary location for the information as it moves from one specialist business activity to another.

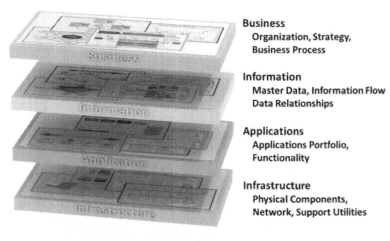

Business
Organization, Strategy,
Business Process

Information
Master Data, Information Flow
Data Relationships

Applications
Applications Portfolio,
Functionality

Infrastructure
Physical Components,
Network, Support Utilities

Figure 52: Levels of Enterprise Architecture in E&P companies

Of the four layers shown here the "Information" one is the least understood. There are numerous IT specialists that are able to provide a detailed understanding of the networks and servers that make up infrastructure. There is no shortage of software vendors that will help identify applications that oil companies should employ. There is even a wide choice of "business consultants" that will discuss asset lifecycles and business activities. However, there is a distinct lack of "information layer" architects that combine an understanding of E&P data with practical experience in implementing the type of integration solutions that are needed.

Key aspects of the information landscape

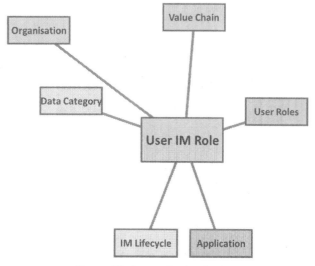

Figure 53: An overly simple view

Understanding the information within an organization requires an agreement about the topics to be characterized. For example, a simplified (indeed, as will be shown, over simplified) map of the main topics is shown above. The original focus of this diagram was to clarify the roles played by users within the information management process, for example what are the responsibilities of the data definition owners.

By reviewing each of these topics in turn and clearly defining what is intended a clearer picture will emerge.

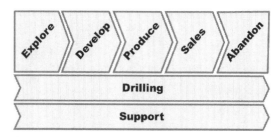

Figure 54: A typical "value chain"

The "Value Chain" is the cycle of business steps that are applied to any oil industry asset. This term is commonly used and widely understood in the industry. Often it is characterized by a set of steps called things like "Explore", "Develop", "Produce" and "Abandon". These stages relate both to departments within the organization, such as the "Exploration Department", and to key decisions, such as the decision to convert an opportunity to a prospect. The "Value Chain" does not have a direct impact on particular data categories, for example drilling data might be crucial for every one of these stages.

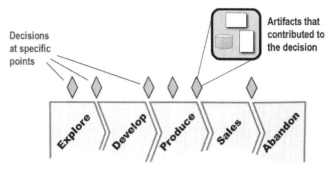

Figure 55: Data is related to business decisions rather than the value chain

Moving an asset from one stage in the value chain to the next usually requires a business decision, which depends on a defined set of deliverable artifacts, such as a report of a prospect's financial viability. So a clear description of the information requires some understanding of the decisions being taken and the deliverables required for them.

The user role, whether they are reservoir engineers, drillers, geophysicists or geologists, does have an influence on their interaction with data. For example, one would expect that the well logs would be published by a petrophysicist, or at least by someone playing that role.

The application being used also has a more nuanced relationship to the information. There are some collections of applications that all share a common database, in this case it is the database that is important, not the individual applications. More subtly, there are some applications that support multiple data sources, for example, some oil companies have two distinct stores for well log data, one for the petrophysicist's day to day work and another to store the "approved" curve data. In this case a single application supports two distinct repositories, each with its own rules about who can load, manipulate and read the data. So, rather than applications, it is the repositories that relate to the information being handled.

The Information Lifecycle typically has stages that are named something like "Identify", "Load", "Validate", "Publish", "Utilize" and "Dispose", these will be explored in some detail in chapter 11 – "Corporate and project data". As that will explain, these activities imply a number of "repository roles" that are a better basis for tracking information within the organization.

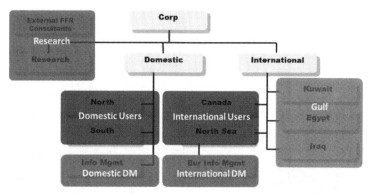

Figure 56: Corporate organization is distinct from data management profile

Any company has an organization that defines reporting and budgetary structures, but, these do not necessarily match the way that data is handled. In the example shown above the company has two distinct departments, "domestic" and "international", users in these two areas employ data in much the same way. In the above case describing data handling within the departments leads to an overly complicated view. Distinguishing two "profiles", one covering data handling by the users and the other by the DM staff simplifies the description.

All discussions about data handling within E&P companies must be aware of the data categories being addressed. Agreeing on a defined set of data groupings must be one of the first tasks to be undertaken. This topic was already explored in chapter 3 – "E&P data for the non-specialist".

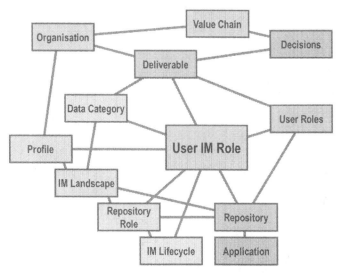

Figure 57: The important concepts for information handling

Taking these clarifications into account delivers a more complete suite of topics that need to be considered. The figure above shows a set of concepts that can form the basis for a more realistic architecture.

Domains & data types

Any discussion of data handling with E&P companies must at some point agree on a list of the data categories and how they are to be considered. One approach that has been tried many times is to start by designing a single consistent model that can accommodate all data. For example, it might be anticipated that all the "important" data should be stored in a single repository. This tactic has been employed by many groups over the years, for example by POSC in the 1990s with their Epicentre data model. Even a vast investment in very experienced resources over the last 20 years has, however, completely failed to achieve this goal.

For the foreseeable future this "single model" approach is almost certainly unachievable. There is no perfect way to characterize the whole range of data that is required for exploration and production. This is actually a much less surprising result than many naïve oil company staff expect.

Success in exploring for hydrocarbons and in maintaining production levels requires a flexible and innovative approach. Over the years oil companies have invested in order to maximize the benefit they achieve from all the disciplines involved, this has often resulted in specialized applications and techniques which employ unique ways of understanding the world. Given the fact that a database table describing a well is just an encapsulation of the aspects that one discipline feels are important it should not be surprising that distinct specialists employ incompatible "logical models".

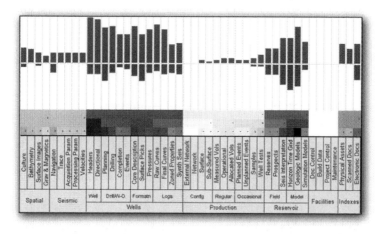

Figure 58: The importance of different data categories in one oil company

The dream of creating a single "logical model" of E&P data may be beyond our grasp, but there is still a benefit from characterizing all the important technical data. In the diagram above, a simple listing of the key data categories was used to measure how often a collection of users "used" (in green above the line) or "edited" (in blue below) different groups of data. Even a cursory glance allows anyone to pick out the data categories that are of greatest importance to this particular group.

The Management of Oil Industry

The fact that the data categories employed are not tied to a single precise data model allows the users to discuss their interactions without getting distracted by the details of implementation. This, in turn, allows the "Enterprise Architect" to document how information flows across discipline boundaries.

This flexible approach can lead to discussions about the precise positioning of different sets of data, for example, seismic checkshots measured down the well could be classified as well based data, seismic data or attributes of the reservoir. An arbitrary agreement to select a single shared view helps to focus the discussion on the more important questions about where this data comes from, what processes manipulate it and who requires those results for further work.

Representing Architecture

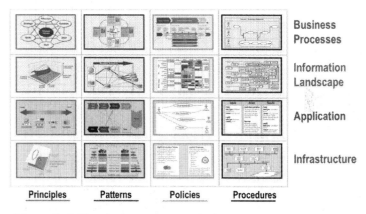

Figure 59: Different pictures help illustrate aspects of the architecture

There are a wide range of different diagrams that can be of assistance when documenting and discussing any architecture. The distinct "layers" in the enterprise each have different focus and so can benefit from employing specialized diagrams. In addition, a depiction that works well for describing an abstract universal principle will typically not be the best way to document a detailed procedure that only applies under a precise set of conditions.

It is valuable to be familiar with many different categories of illustrative diagram, this will make it more likely that when a situation must be illustrated there is an appropriate picture that can help illuminate the point being made. Of course, there are an almost infinite variety of potential pictures that could prove valuable.

This section picks out a few of the most widely applicable forms that have proved valuable when addressing information concerns in the past.

Matrix Views

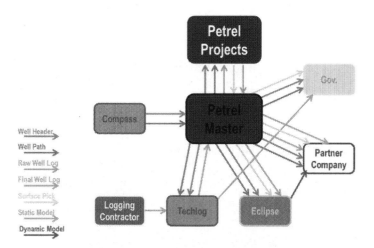

Figure 60: Data flows related to a single repository

The figure above uses a "boxes and arrows" type diagram to illustrate how data flows into and out of a single repository, the "Petrel Master". Various categories of data are obtained from different sources and dispatched to other locations, but, this picture doesn't illustrate where the "approved" versions of data are to be found, where data is manipulated and interpreted or which components are outside the control of the organization.

The Management of Oil Industry

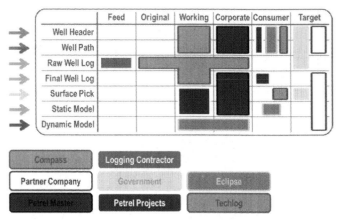

Figure 61: A "matrix" version of the same flows

If the same data flows are shown using the roles described later (in chapter 11) in a "matrix picture" then all these shortcomings are removed. This type of illustration requires a small amount of additional experience to interpret, but the result is more precise in meaning, more systematic in layout and easier to keep updated.

Activity Diagram

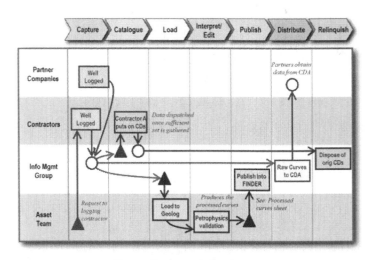

Figure 62: An activity diagram

Activity diagrams are a specialized form of swim-lane diagram. They show the actions (shown by rectangular boxes), the requests dispatched (shown by triangles) and those received (shown by circles) in an overall process. Each actor is listed down the side and the overall process is shown across the top. Groups of related activities can be conveyed by color and free form notes explain key points.

By imposing some strict rules, for example, that all inter-actor communication must either start or end with a request, they force the diagram's author to articulate the communications between those involved. Often an attempt to create a consistent and clear activity diagram will quickly identify the key communication issues and misunderstood actions.

UML

The Unified Modeling Language[24] (UML) from Rational is a graphical formalism that has been widely used across a number of industries. UML was originally developed as a way to document software. However it has proved to be invaluable for documenting many types of system, especially relating to business workflows and activities.

Unfortunately, this popularity has led to a widespread use of "almost UML" diagrams. The best of these decide not to follow UML conventions in order to help illuminate a particular point, the worst of them seem to believe that any old combination of boxes and arrows will be impressive enough. Such diagrams often convey less meaning than at first seems apparent.

UML defines nine different types of diagram, the structural diagrams:

- **Class:** Shows a set of classes, interfaces, collaborations and their relationships
- **Object:** A set of objects and their relationships

---

[24] There are many good reference books on UML, for example "The Unified Modelling Language User Guide – Second Edition" by Brooch, Rumbaugh & Jacobson ISBN 978-0321267979

- **Component:** shows the various components and their relationships
- **Deployment:** shows nodes and their relationships

And the behavioral diagrams:

- **Use Case:** shows actors and their relationships
- **Sequence:** emphasizing the time ordering of messages
- **Collaboration:** that emphasizes the structural organization of communicating objects
- **Statechart:** that emphasizes the event ordered behavior of an object
- **Activity:** that shows a state machine emphasizing the flow from activity to activity

RACI

	Asset Manager	Petrophysicist	Geologist	Vendor
Measure	I	C		RA
Deliver CD		IA		R
Log Splice		RA		
Log Correct		RA	C	
Publish Log	A	R	I	

Responsible, **A**ccountable, **C**onsulted, **I**nformed

Figure 63: An example RACI diagram

A RACI diagram lists all the actors and the various activities in a grid. For each combination it asserts which of the participants is Responsible, Accountable, Consulted or Informed. The CAIRO versions extend the list to include those that are to be **O**mitted from the activity.

This simple diagram makes it very easy to document the responsibilities of those involved. It is a valuable tool to apply early when change is required.

Chevrons

One overly used representation is the set of chevrons. A number of examples of this type of sequence have already been discussed, such as the value chain and information lifecycle diagrams. The message being conveyed is that the described process is like an assembly line, it has a well-defined order and a clear set of interfaces between the steps. Where the process being described is a "conveyor belt" of steps this is a good metaphor to employ, using it in other situations can just add confusion.

Zachman Framework

The Zachman framework[25] consists of a matrix of pictures each focused on a single aspect of the overall system.

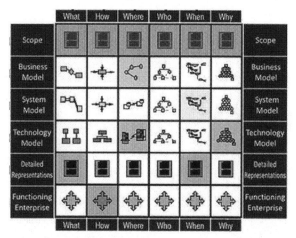

Figure 64: The Zachman Framework

The columns each focus on a single aspect: data; function; network; people; time; and motivation. The rows on an activity: scope; business model; system model; technology; architecture; and enterprise. Each intersection inspires a number of concerns, questions and pictures.

---

[25] The initial description was in "A Framework for Information Systems Architecture" by John Zachman published in 1987 as an article in the IBM Systems journal, various updates have been made since, for example at http://www.zachman.com/

8. Data Development

The term "develop" has a different specific meaning within the context of oil industry activities. Oilfields are described as going through three phases, exploration, development and production. In this case the word is being used to describe the creation of tools and techniques to manipulate data, rather than the more industrial use of the term prevalent in the wider oil industry.

All large organizations are forced to create capabilities to manipulate data. In many industries this extends to fashioning the applications and defining the data repositories. Most oil companies came to the realization that external specialized vendors were able to generate more effective tools for interpreting subsurface data than their own in-house developers could manage, at least for most activities. As a result, the main reason oil companies have to create software is in order to integrate components from a range of external vendors, rather than when developing their own custom built applications.

Running projects

There are a number of widely employed project management methodologies, for example PRINCE2 and PMI. The most widely used ones have quite similar features, a focus on the business case, formal tracking of stages and reporting by exception.

Any development projects undertaken for oil companies will usually be expected to be conducted in accordance with a recognized project management methodology. There are numerous excellent courses, books and web resources available and oil industry project management does not significantly differ from other computer based system development.

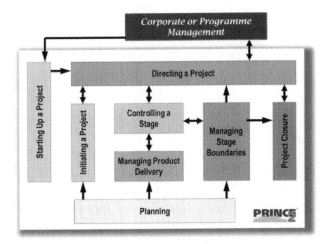

Figure 65: PRINCE2 is a project management methodology

For example, PRINCE2 defines eight "processes" that all projects have to implement, using "components" and "techniques" that define all the artifacts, roles and tasks that are required.

Change Management

For many improvement projects the most important single factor determining success is the ability to persuade the target users to modify the way they work. Change Management is an approach to help stakeholders to accept and embrace changes in their business environment.

Stakeholders

Wake-up

Ability

Review

Measure

Figure 66: Change management focuses on people

There are a number of different change management methodologies that can be applied, they mostly have similar goals and approaches. It is important to select a methodology and apply it consistently, rather than to worry about which one has been selected. One approach is to divide the change process into five stages:

- **Stakeholders** – identify the key participants including the sponsors, target groups and trainers. Draw the sponsorship diagram
- **Wake-up** – Deliver the material to explain the change and instill desire in the participants. Success for this stage is measured by the wish for change, not the ability to implement it
- **Ability** – Training and practice in the new activities, best delivered by the immediate manager of each profile group
- **Review** – Survey the target users to measure: understanding; desire; adoption; and proficiency. Adjust the project to address the most pressing issues
- **Measure** – Define metrics to assess the effectiveness of the change and measure them

The participants can be characterized by their attitude to the change (pro, neutral or anti), their capability (veteran, experienced, qualified or rookie) and their involvement in the project (constant, by request or occasional).

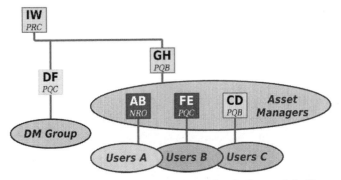

Figure 67: A sponsorship diagram identifies the key stakeholders

The understanding of the relationships between groups, sponsors and other participants can then be summarized in a "sponsorship diagram" that helps plan and review the change project. This documents the various individual participants and groups and shows how they can be influenced.

The integration spectrum

For a variety of reasons, suites of E&P applications that focused on delivering integrated sets of tools have never become commercially successful in the oil industry. Up to now there has been an emphasis on purchasing the "best in class" tool for each domain, usually initially created by a vendor that specialized in honing capabilities for a focused group of users. This means that many oil companies find that their main data development activity is constructing paths to bridge between applications that come from different sources.

There are a range of approaches to integration and, also, a number of ways to compare between them. One useful classification scheme is to think of integration solutions as occurring along a "spectrum"[26].

---

[26] This approach follows that described in "The Data Integration Spectrum" presented at AAPG Cairo in 2002 by Steve Hawtin, Najib Abusalbi, Lester Bayne & Mark Chidwick

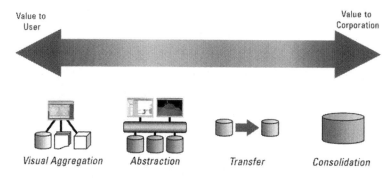

Value to
User

Value to
Corporation

Visual Aggregation   Abstraction   Transfer   Consolidation

Figure 68: There are a range of strategies for implementing integration

At one extreme there are approaches that merely display information from multiple sources, performing the integration only visually. The opposite approach is to migrate all the available data from multiple sources into a consistent structure, such as a single relational database. In general the implementation cost increases dramatically from left to right, so do the benefits. Having all the available data in a single consolidated database makes later processing and manipulation much simpler.

Visual Aggregation

Visual Aggregation brings the data together on the user's display without attempting to validate it through business rules. For example, GIS and "web portal" solutions allow the user to relate information from a range of sources that have no clearly defined underlying connection.

This approach has the advantage that it does not require complex processes to confirm data consistency before it can be applied. This usually results in a more up-to-date set of information being available, often a crucial element in the success of the solution. In addition it can provide a good mechanism for relating "higher level" business objects, without being slowed down by the "technical details" that can often make less flexible approaches more expensive to implement.

This flexibility comes at a price in that data that is integrated this way does not lend itself to further processing. While visual integration helps provide a high level summary it does not assist in enforcing consistency or in later automated processing, such as quality checks.

Abstraction

Abstraction provides an intermediate layer that isolates the viewer from the details of information that is obtained from a variety of locations. This is normally achieved by simplifying the actual data using a more abstract set of "business objects".

In Visual Aggregation there are no constraints placed on the data that is accessible. Under Abstraction, in contrast, it is important that there is consistency in the way entities are identified in the various data sources. The system must be able to recognize two different renditions of "the same" real world business object. Abstraction leads to integration solutions that are powerful and can be easy to install. Some processing on the data can be carried out, although normally performance requirements constrain this to just the most commonly used attributes.

It is often complex to create the "Data Adaptors" that mediate between the abstraction framework and the external data sources. This is especially true where local conventions change the way that data is stored. In addition, the generic object definition provided by the framework can never meet the needs of all the possible applications.

Even when it is possible to run applications that can extract information from many possible sources there will normally be good business reasons for restricting how the abstraction system is applied. For example, if the company's business processes define the location where approved well headers are to be found then the abstraction system should probably be prevented from obtaining them from alternate non-approved locations.

One of the advantages of this approach is that the management of data is kept closer to the data sources. This implies that other tactics are required to fulfill the more traditional data management tasks.

Transfer

Transfer performs the classic extract, transform, load (ETL) sequence to copy data from where it is to where it needs to be. At the moment this is the most widely adopted approach to data integration and can support any complexity of data flow.

The main advantage of this approach is that it can apply any transformation to the data as part of the copying process. This is just as well, since the data must conform exactly with the restraints of the target before it can be successfully inserted. The main disadvantage of this approach is that it can apply any transformation to the data as part of the copying process, which makes tracking what was done quite challenging.

Transfer approaches can bring together data from a wide variety of locations, making this the only viable way to integrate certain legacy and proprietary data sources. For some kinds of data, such as off-line information, there is no option but to duplicate the data via a transfer.

The data being transferred can also be captured in a format-independent form for archiving and transmission to remote locations. The view of the transfer can be easily tailored to the end-user's requirements, showing only those aspects that are important.

However, even with all these advantages, the transfer approach does of course lead to data duplication, with all the well-known difficulties that this implies.

Consolidation

The most precise form of integration is to consolidate all the data into a single repository. If information is available from a single consistent location it simplifies the task of subsequent processing as well as making logical groupings of data readily available for a wide range of applications. This approach makes the later task of data management much easier. For example, with a single trusted location the management of entitlements is simplified. By having a single "master" location the difficulties of data duplication are also eliminated.

The difficulty with this approach is primarily the cost due to: the effort it takes to initially implement; the complexity of transforming the data; and the time involved in first carrying out the necessary data quality checks. In addition, there are categories of information that cannot readily be made to fit into a single repository in an effective way, leading to the holding of data in a form that does not readily meet the needs of applications or omitting some essential related or contextual information.

Defining data standards

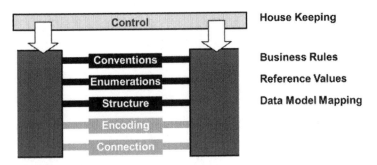

Figure 69: There are a range of strategies for implementing integration

When looking at the way any particular piece of integration is to be implemented it is valuable to consider the different levels at which communication must be defined. These concerns often relate to the elements listed in the figure above.

When transferring data, for example, the questions that must be answered are:

- **Connection:** How will the two systems physically connect, for example will they be running in the same machine or network?
- **Encoding:** What format will be used to represent the data elements, will floating point numbers be IEEE, DEC or ASCII strings, how will different components be flagged?
- **Structure:** What entities will be allowed, what attributes will be mandatory?
- **Enumerations:** Which attributes have limitations on potential values, for example a "partner company" field that must contain entries from a defined list? Where are the valid values found?
- **Conventions:** There are always inherent usually undocumented relationships between data elements
- **Control:** One essential element that is often neglected is that of controlling the process

Connection

With modern systems there is less need to worry about this level. In past decades one would have to employ special cables, cross-over adaptors and Kermit to connect to the target system. For most modern systems a standard TCP/IP stack (or possibly a physical USB stick) does all that is required to get the data where it is needed.

Of course those using SCADA and real-time data do not have such an easy time.

Encoding

Encoding standards are also becoming much less of an issue. In the past careful examination of hex dump printouts would be

---

Exploration & Production Data   93

required to unpick the combination of EBCDIC text strings, customized floating point formats and highly packed bit vectors. File size is much less of a concern than it used to be, which means that ASCII based formats are appropriate for most purposes. The widespread adoption of one particular ASCII based encoding, that is XML, make that the obvious choice for most requirements.

In 1991 the American Petroleum Institute (API) published a description of an encoding for digital data, called "API Recommended Practice 66"[27] widely known as RP66. It formed the underlying basis for a number of other standards such as Geoshare, WITS and DLIS. While its use these days is fairly restricted there are some specialized oil industry formats that still employ it.

Structure

Probably the best way to clarify structure is through the creation of a data model that defines the entities and relationships involved. There are a number of ways to precisely define the elements of data model, from UML diagrams to specialized languages such as EXPRESS.

ANSI suggested that data models can be divided into four forms:

- **External Schemas**: a collection of proposed elements obtained from different stakeholders, may be inconsistent and incomplete
- **Conceptual Schema**: a consolidated set of requirements, will be consistent but may not be complete
- **Logical Model**: a complete and consistent description of all the elements, may require further clarification in order to be implementable

---

[27] The definition of the various versions of RP66 are available from Energistics as part of the standards they publish for example at http://www.energistics.org/geosciences/geology-standards

- **Physical Model**: a data model that can be directly applied within a particular technology, for example a DDL file within an SQL based DBMS

Enumeration

Within a particular structure there are often attributes that are only allowed to take on a limited number of values. This could be, for example: a list of countries in the world; a list of available pipe diameters; a list of partner companies; or any other restricted set of values. The key to successfully handling such definitions is to maintain a clear description of what is being covered, a widely publicized list of acceptable values, a known process to update the list and a mechanism for flagging potential new values that are not yet on the accepted list.

The creation of definitive lists of reference values will be explored when "Information Architecture" is more fully discussed in chapter 13 – "Document Management".

Conventions

In any real collection of data there will be a number of "unwritten" conventions that impose further constraints on the way the data works. This is usually the reason why two systems that both follow the same standards generally won't work together as well as one might expect. The inherent ambiguity within a particular structure or reference values set generally only becomes apparent when two different interpretations are compared and contrasted.

Control

The exercise of control is the most widely distinct element in the whole stack. For example, it is important to understand whether data is synchronized automatically during the night or by a manual process. Since there are few widely adopted formalisms for describing when an activity should occur this will usually remain an informal aspect of the integration process.

9. Data Operations

Most oil companies don't follow a strictly prescribed order for data handling operations. Successful organizations combine evidence in all sorts of inventive new ways to make discoveries that have eluded their competitors. Restricting the users to only following set patterns is seen as an ineffective way to control the overall process. In contrast, efficiently delivering clearly prescribed services is the key to cost effective data management. Finding a workable compromise between the flexibility of the overall flows and the precision of standardized procedures is the goal of many data management departments.

ITIL

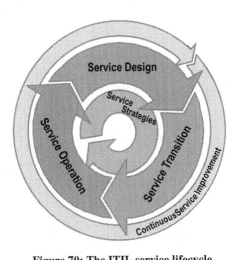

Figure 70: The ITIL service lifecycle

The ITIL standard was originally created to describe the activities of a typical IT department, it is also an effective way to formally document the services provided by the data management function.

Adopting recognized standards such as ITIL helps ensure that best practices are employed, but, the decision to employ this type of formalized approach can sometimes pose as many questions as it answers. In particular, there is a need to create a "Service

Catalogue" that formally defines all the activities to be conducted. How are these services to be identified? Creating a comprehensive directory of all data handling services is always a time consuming business. It can only really be justified when there are many distinct locations that can employ it or where the service is being provided by a clearly distinct group that need to clarify their activities.

Who handles the data activities?

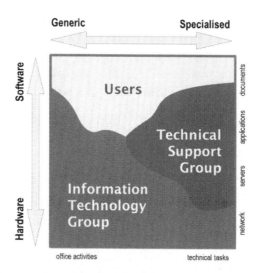

Figure 71: Responsibility is often divided between groups

In many oil companies the responsibility for supporting technology is divided between the generalist IT group, the end users and some kind of specialist group focused on supporting the domain specific data, software and hardware. The exact composition of these specialist groups varies, often they are an amalgamation of departments reporting to the Chief Information Officer, support staff within the assets and external service vendors. Different oil companies also vary in where they place the dividing line. Some companies assign responsibility for all hardware to the generic IT group, while others perceive the provision of, for example, specialist compute servers for simulation to be outside their competency.

10. Data Security

Information security is a crucial aspect of modern life. There are many scare stories about identity theft and the dangers of public disclosure of private information. When dealing with oil companies the levels of financial impact make many of them very worried about potential threats.

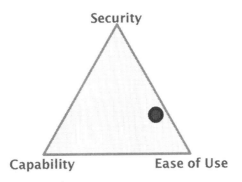

Figure 72: There is a balance between security and capability

Security is never the only concern, the most secure system would be one that no-one could ever use. For a given implementation cost a system can select between three opposing options, adding to the capabilities, making access simpler or being more secure. Generally reducing the constraints a system imposes will make it more valuable but less secure.

Working out the most appropriate balance between making an easy to access system and locking down all potential leaks requires a review of the potential financial and other costs that a breach would deliver.

There are two main different security risks that always need to be considered:

- Allowing access to information to someone who should not have it

- Preventing access to information for someone that is entitled to it

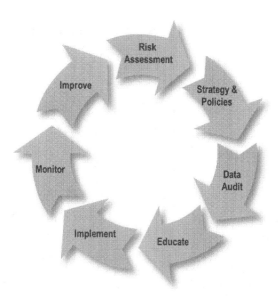

Figure 73: Identifying potential risks is the first step

Assessing risks requires that a realistic assessment of the impact must be included. If a competitor becomes aware of a discovery and licenses all the nearby leases the financial implications can be enormous. In contrast, if a national oil company loses control of the same information it could be that no competitor can benefit because the country's laws ensure that the company have to participate in any future development anyway.

Defining realistic security policies is another area that many companies struggle with. A recent breach in a large national oil company was identified as originating in the use of personal USB memory sticks, the immediate response was to prevent such devices from being used. This caused an immense disruption as so many business processes relied on the easy transport of documents and presentations into and out of the organization. It forced the users to send all data via email, file transfers and downloads from the internet, thus exposing the organization to a much wider and less controllable set of risks. A more considered policy could have retained some capability to handle USB based data and provided a more controlled way of bringing data in.

Experienced information security experts highlight "social engineering" as the most successful form of attack. This relies on tricking ordinary users into breaching security through an apparently innocent action. Opening an image within an email, for example, might reveal key identity information which can be exploited in a later attack.

The security audit is an essential tool to harden any organization against attack. Usually this would involve specialist reviewers examining the systems being employed and attempting to identify vulnerabilities. Often those involved in specifying or operating the existing systems are the least able to realistically appraise its weaknesses.

Ensuring future access

One often overlooked aspect of data security is ensuring that information continues to be available to those that have rights to it. The provision of back-ups is one way to address this, but, within oil companies a lot of data becomes inaccessible through being labeled incorrectly or being accidently placed in the wrong location.

Information Security v Facility Security

The security of information is built on the physical restrictions placed on the systems involved, if a supposedly secure location can be entered just by walking up to the security door carrying an apparently heavy box then laptops or even servers holding crucial data are liable to go missing.

The fact that a facility is secure does not mean that vigilance in validating identities can be overlooked. A security professional will be aware of the information flows as well as the infrastructure and physical aspects of their systems.

11. Corporate and project data

In the DMBoK this topic has been called "Reference and Master Data Management", and the description is focused on the creation and management of "Master" data stores in formal databases. In E&P the divisions between reference data, meta-data, business intelligence and document management that are a standard approach in most industries do not really apply. There would be no consensus between E&P disciplines as to which items fall into each of these categories. This is why this function has been renamed in this description.

The concept of an integrated "Master" set of E&P data has been the subject of heated discussion for at least the last 20 years. Many companies, vendors and industry associations have at some point attempted to implement a single technical system able to manage the complete range of important E&P structured data, these efforts have consistently failed to deliver the anticipated benefits. As a result there is an understandable caution about using the phrase "Master Data" without qualifying its exact meaning.

Information lifecycle & roles

Figure 74: One possible Information Lifecycle

Having a consistent set of names for the activities involved in handling information is, as has already been discussed, a crucial part of understanding the overall data lifecycle. Adopting a view of the information flows based on activities helps to document the services that the business requires to handle its data.

The need to clearly define what each of these task names actually mean is obvious. An outline of the activities implied by the names shown in Figure 74 has been provided later in this chapter, before

---

this can be fully described it will be necessary to explore the closely related topic of "repository roles".

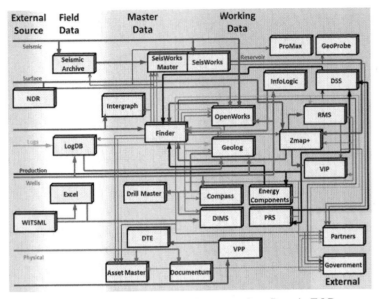

Figure 75: The wrong way to document data flows in E&P

When it comes to documenting how all the various data sources are connected within even the smallest E&P company there is one obvious approach. That is to draw a big diagram which contains all the key repositories and shows how different data categories of data flow using directional lines.

In many industries this is the optimal way to document which data stores are important and to show how the key data flows within the organization. When these types of "data flow diagrams" are drawn for E&P companies there are just too many repositories, too many data categories and too many connections. This type of diagram used to be common in oil company data management departments, almost every one of them missed out important sources, had dangling links and impossible loops.

There is a valid role for the data flow diagram. When a restricted set of data is being considered, for example, when looking at the flow of well curve data, it is possible to have a depiction that does simplify the picture and within this constrained situation it is possible for a small team to validate all the connections.

Repository Roles

So, given that the "information landscape" is too complex to render using a conventional data flow diagram how should this type of understanding be created?

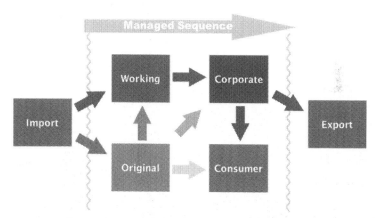

Figure 76: The roles that different repositories play

Focusing on a small group of "repository roles" enables the creation of relatively simple pictures to discuss data flows. The actual particular list of repository roles employed is of less importance than the fact that such roles are identified and consistently utilized. Rather than using contentious terms such as "Master Data" the six roles defined here are a better match to the way repositories are really used within most oil companies:

- **Import:** Where data enters the control of the organization
- **Original Data:** Where unedited copies of externally sourced data is kept for future reference
- **Working Area:** Where data is corrected, edited or created
- **Corporate Data:** Where the approved, official version is to be found

- **Data Consumer:** Where data is used but not modified
- **Export:** Where data is delivered outside the organization

Import (External Source)

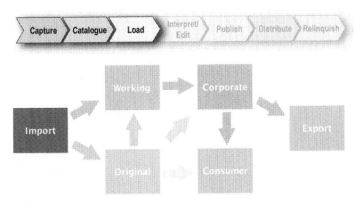

Figure 77: Activities that employ the import role

Within any organization there are sets of data that come from outside. Typically this data will come from contractors, the government or partner companies that are operating a field. As the figure above illustrates the three activities of Capture, Catalogue and Load interact with the Import repository role.

Original Data

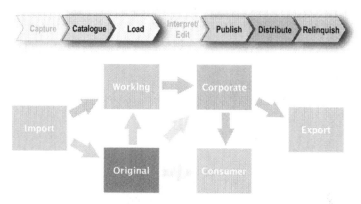

Figure 78: Activities that employ the original data role

All data is liable to correction. When corrections are made it is valuable to have a complete history, including a copy of the data exactly as it was supplied to the organization.

As an example when the volume of oil produced by well "15C" over the course of a single day is faxed back to the office someone might realize that there is no such well. They might assume that the report was meant to relate to well "16C" and correct the values as they are typed in to the system. If some time later someone realizes that well "16C" was inactive at the time and the record was actually referring to the well "15E" then correcting the data will be simplified if there is a record of the original mistaken value.

Working Area

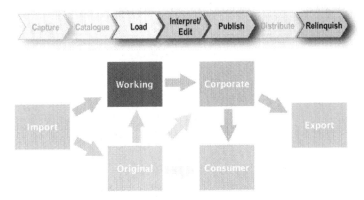

Figure 79: Activities that employ the working data role

Generally, the experts in a particular domain will have a "sandbox" area where they can try out various hypotheses in order to identify the one they feel best fits the evidence available. For example, the structural modelers will have an application that lets them compare various potential subsurface geometries to see how well each one fits the seismic interpretation and well measurements.

The most effective of these "working areas" have a number of properties in common:

- **Powerful:** the tools available encourage the users to test out many different possibilities providing the ability to quickly add potential concepts
- **Unrestrained:** the ability to incorporate inputs from a wide variety of sources in a flexible way without overly worrying about where that data "should fit"
- **Private:** the space is used for "brain storming" new concepts and then testing them, this is easier if it is done behind closed doors
- **Ambiguous:** often there is a need to hold multiple different potential concepts while the specialists contrasts them in order to identify the best combination

Once the professional has tested out a range of possible interpretations and selected the one they feel best fits they will generally "publish" this to the rest of the organization. However while they are working on a new set of concepts the last thing they want is for the data management group to restrict their freedom to test ideas.

Corporate Data

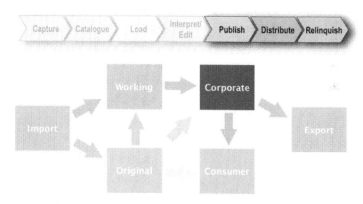

Figure 80: Activities that employ the corporate data role

Once a conclusion is reached about a particular domain by one group it often needs to be shared by other experts. For example once a static subsurface model has been created by the Geologist it will be needed by the Reservoir Engineer, to create a dynamic model and by the Financial Analyst, to deliver reserves estimates.

The typical consumer of this type of data does not want to have to delve into details in order to understand the interpretation, they just want to be presented with the "best current understanding" in a way that suites their needs (rather than in the form that matched the producer's processes). So a "single version of the truth" is selected reviewed and made available to as many potential users as possible.

This data is stored in a location that ideally has the following properties:

- **Public:** a location that is both widely known and accessible to everyone that could potentially want the information (assuming they are entitled to see it)
- **Unique:** a single version of the truth that should be employed by all consumers, until it is later updated
- **Audited:** a complete history of this "official" version, so that queries can be resolved
- **Precise:** every component must be exactly labeled so users of the information know what they can do with it

Notice that these properties are usually not determined by the particular technology, but rather by the combination of business needs and activities. For example, an Excel spread-sheet could be used to provide a precise definition of the allocated production of all wells, but only if it follows a particular layout of the columns, ensures all volumes are defined in the same units and holds values that have been checked and approved for widespread use.

It is not unusual for oil companies to employ the same applications to both work on data and to distribute it across the organization. This can be an effective way of working, but only if the "distributed results" follow a process that is precise, audited, and reviewed. Just providing widespread access to the area where data is being actively worked on, without clearly labeling which of the various versions are to be used, ensures that often the wrong one will be employed. Also allowing users to actively modify the "best current understanding" makes it impossible to review past decisions within the context of what was known at the time.

Data Consumer

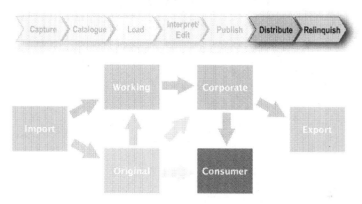

Figure 81: Activities that employ the data consumer role

If someone wishes to just utilize a piece of data, without any thought of modifying it, then they can be considered a "data consumer". This pattern is quite easy to deal with, as long as the user has some way to obtain the data what they do with it has no effect on anyone else. As far as the rest of the organization is concerned the fact that this user receives data for their own purposes makes them a "sink" for this category of data.

An example would be well logs, the petrophysicist is responsible for placing them into an accessible shared location. The many users of those curves will each load them into their own tool and apply them in their own processes. If they identify something they don't like ideally they won't modify the corporate data, they will explain their concern to the data owner (the petrophysicist) and ask them to fix the issue.

The fact that this data is consumed simplifies its handling, as long as there is an effective way to distribute the data, the information management team don't need to be concerned with what the consumer does with the data later.

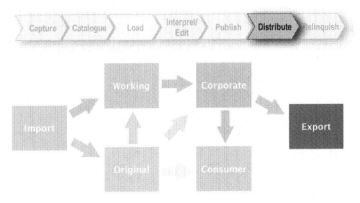

Figure 82: Activities that employ the export role

The final repository role is concerned with data that is sent out from the organization. In oil companies this is usually sending data to partner companies or government agencies.

The dispatch of data should be a major concern for any E&P company. This is not just because of the security implications, but more importantly because data is only usually sent out when there is a legal obligation involved. This means that recording which data was sent, who validated it, where it was sent to and so on can become incredibly important when later questions arise.

In larger organizations there are formal paths whereby any data sent externally must be registered and documented. This is usually only imposed after an incident. One example occurred when a user copied a geological model to a partner, without realizing that it incorporated a regional seismic interpretation that the partner was not entitled to.

The information lifecycle

By imposing a single abstract data lifecycle on each data category it becomes easier to ensure consistency in the way different departments behave. Another benefit is that because the classification is more systematic it becomes possible to identify missing procedures that have not yet been written.

Figure 83: One possible "Data Lifecycle"

There are many variants on the "Information Lifecycle" one of the most commonly used ones is shown in the figure above. As long as an oil company is consistent in applying the terms the particular details are not usually crucial.

A clear understanding of the repository roles makes it simpler to describe the appropriate characteristics of each activity. As has already been outlined, it is important that a consistent set of activities and repository roles are employed. Here are a set of definitions of the lifecycle activities that complies with the roles explained above.

Capture

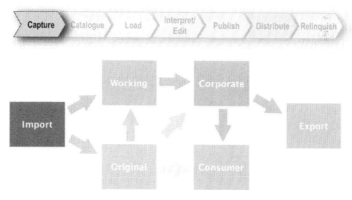

Figure 84: Roles involved in the "capture" activity

When data is first identified it often needs to be documented before it is available, for example when a well is to be logged or when the "value of information" is being discussed for a potential new seismic survey.

Catalogue

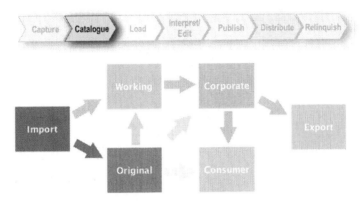

Figure 85: Roles involved in the "catalogue" activity

When data is supplied by an external source it is often noted, indexed and archived in its original form. This process is quite distinct from "loading" the data since the goal is to keep a record of exactly what was delivered rather than interpreting it in any way.

Load

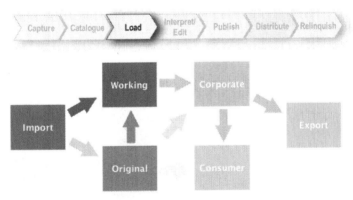

Figure 86: Roles involved in the "load" activity

Data must be loaded into a system in order to allow it to be reviewed, corrected or adjusted. This process of "loading" the data generally places it into a working or staging area so that, if necessary, it can be fixed.

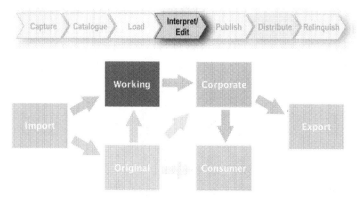

Figure 87: Roles involved in the "interpret" activity

The process of adjusting the data should only take place within a working area. Many companies divide this activity into a number of more finely defined phases:

- **Validate/ Check:** check that the data conforms with company standards and expected conventions
- **Create/ Interpret:** when data originates within the organization rather than being loaded from an external source. This often involves interpreting some other category of data, for example picking well tops from log curves
- **Modify/ Edit:** when data requires some adjustment, for example when log curves need to be depth matched and spliced

The "validate" step may be assigned to data technicians rather than the domain experts. Other than this, most of the activities that manipulate the data within the working area are wholly controlled by the specialist users.

Publish

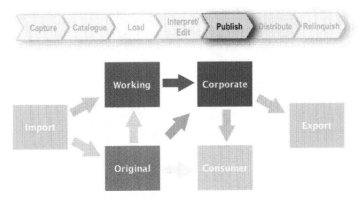

Figure 88: Roles involved in the "publish" activity

The process of taking results and making them available for other users to exploit is usually given a name like "publish". If the corporate standards expect shared data to have been "approved" this step is the obvious place to have the data reviewed.

Distribute

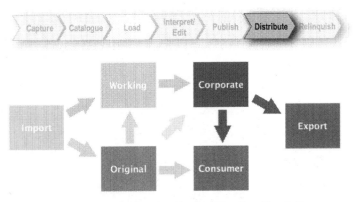

Figure 89: Roles involved in the "distribute" activity

Once data is available in the shared location it will need to be distributed in some way. The activity of distributing data will usually require some validation of entitlements, especially when the target is external to the organization.

Relinquish

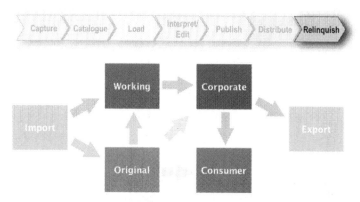

Figure 90: Roles involved in the "relinquish" activity

This stage in the data lifecycle is the one that is most often forgotten. In most E&P companies data is only relinquished under special circumstances, for example when an asset is sold. When this occurs there should be a formal process to ensure that every instance of the affected data is removed from all the company's systems, in practice this process is almost never completed.

In some countries the obligation to hold data related to particular assets, such as wells, continues "forever". In practice this legal constraint can be passed on by selling the asset to another party, in which case they take over the obligation. Alternatively there may be a recognized process, such as delivering all the data to a "National Data Centre" that relieves the company of the obligation.

12. Physical data management

The handling of physical data is one of the more unusual features of E&P data management. Most industries have to cope with storing some physical items, but they normally do so with the hope that they never have to go back to them. For example, the storage of signed contracts is justified by their potential to provide evidence in future legal proceedings, most businesses would rather not get involved in future law cases, the physical items provide some level of hedge against this risk.

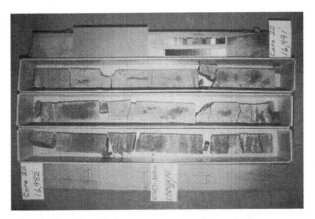

Figure 91: Core samples

The oil industry of course has its share of physical documents that are stored in the hope they are never going to be needed. There are also a wide range of other physical items that are kept in the expectation that they will be valuable in the future, for example:

- **Core Samples:** a wide range of different physical samples are obtained during well drilling and production processes, from core samples stored in boxes to fluid samples in laboratories
- **Documents:** professional journals and historical information such as maps are commonly kept
- **Seismic Tapes:** some data is so voluminous that it is not cost effective to keep copies of it on-line

- **Historic data:** some data is old enough that it was originally delivered in hardcopy form, for example geological maps

Relationship to document management

Many E&P organizations combine "physical data management" with "document management" and, indeed there is a degree of overlap between the two. There are also important differences, the first issue with any physical data management is the ability to locate the actual artifact. In some cases this requires that items are labeled with a physical bar codes or RFID tags.

Figure 92: Physical well logs stored in an oil company's offices

Most of the historical data could never be re-obtained, for example wells that were logged when first drilled cannot be re-measured after being completed. In the North Sea it is not unusual to find that physical well logs taken in the 1970s can still continue to provide valuable insights forty years later.

There are a number of specialized companies that will manage physical data in external warehouses. Often through acquisition a single oil company will find that it owns a range of contracts that hold items in disparate locations. Consolidating these may, or may not, be justified by the business benefits.

All E&P companies will also have a range of important physical data held in their own offices. This may be indexed and registered, although normally it will be managed in a very informal way.

13. Document Management

The importance of documents within the upstream oil industry has been so great that one wit suggested that E&P really stands for Excel & PowerPoint. Crucial data is commonly to be found in vast spread-sheets and often the only evidence that an important piece of data ever existed is the presence of a screen shot in a presentation.

Of course users will often prefer to use spread-sheets to manipulate large groups of numbers without having to specify exactly what they each mean, they can perform any calculation without being constrained by the software's understanding of what makes sense. If you want to multiply the height of members of staff by the geological ages of reservoirs the spread-sheet will allow the calculation (provided you have access to that data). From the point of view of corporate data management the challenge that Excel poses comes from exactly the features that make it so attractive for users.

In most oil companies the various domain experts have been given the freedom to identify for themselves which information is relevant to a particular interpretation. This is based on the valid assumption that by the time a geoscientist is contributing to significant business decisions they are the best people to decide on the part played by each element. This has led to a situation where important aspects of interpretations emerge from documents, discussions and data that each expert considers "personal". Many of these critical elements are stored in informal ways, for example, on the user's private directories or on user's USB drives.

In the better managed environments a proportion of these files will be stored in a more widely accessible location, such as on a shared drive or within a formal "Document Management System". Hopefully these will be the most trustworthy and best described documents.

The most important aspect of any document management system is the ability of the users to identify, locate, extract and use the elements they need to do their jobs.

Searching unstructured data

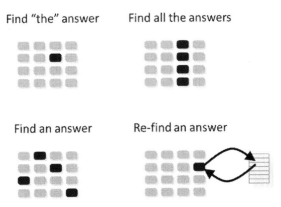

Figure 93: Four different finding strategies

Searching any collection of data generally follows one of four different modes, depending on the reason for the search. For some data, for example listing a contact's phone number, there is a single definitive answer that should be located. If one is searching a legal library to identify relevant cases then it is important that every matching document is identified, otherwise the opposing lawyer will be able to take advantage of your negligence. When browsing to find connected data one might not know if the desired data exists, often in this case it is sufficient to find something that is interesting. Finally, when you are aware of some information, for example, a paper that you reviewed that later turns out to be significant to a new task, you might need to re-find something.

Each of these four user tasks imposes different constraints on the system being employed. In the first case, there must be some kind of identifier, or collection of them, that can be used to track down the information. In the second case, there must be a categorization scheme that ensures complete coverage of all the items being searched. In the final case, some combination of features of the data, such as the author's name or publication date must narrow down the search space. Notice that in this final case the way an item is tracked down might have very little bearing on the reason it is being sought, you might remember that a paper was presented in Vienna because of the long conversation you had with the author about Brazilian gas fields while enjoying sachertorte.

Why Google won't work here

Google have become incredibly successful by implementing a system that uses the textual contents of documents to generate search tags. Their systems examine more than a trillion web pages to build up an index, this ensures that any strange turn of phrase or unusual word will be represented by at least a few exemplars. In addition they invented the "PageRank" algorithm employed to promote the most highly regarded items to place at the top of the list. The consequences of this is that the search for pages containing, for example the three randomly selected words "gaunt", "wordy", and "wrack" delivers more than 50,000 results. Given that most users are looking for "something relevant" there is a good change that one of the first ten things Google selects from this cornucopia will be somewhat related, interesting and usable.

The fact that Google's approach works so well when there are so many potential candidates does not mean that it will function as well when the number of documents is merely in the hundreds of thousands. With less than a millionth of the number of contenders there is a much higher chance that the exact terms used won't precisely match. If the document's author used the term "constrict" but the searcher uses "compress", "squeeze", "contract", "restrict", "constrain", "check", "narrow", "shrink", "attenuate", "cramp", "pinch", "clench" or "tighten" then the document won't be found.

It is this plethora of potential words that works in Google's favor when searching for "something interesting" on the web. There are just so many source documents that whatever terms are used are bound to match some of them.

When searching for either "the answer" or for "all the answers" amongst the relatively smaller volumes of technical documents managed by even the largest oil company the richness of natural language works against achieving reasonable results.

Information Architecture

There is an approach that will deliver the types of search performance that E&P companies require. This relatively new field is known as "Information Architecture" and combines insights from Library Science, Computer Science, Usability Research and Enterprise Architecture. The exact definition of the topic is the subject of some current debate, but the key elements are quite clear.

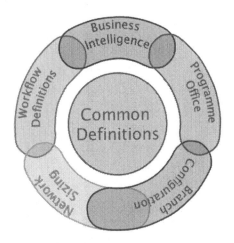

Figure 94: A shared set of definitions can coordinate many activities

There are many different ways to organize an understanding of any complex topic, often these come down to a fixed set of steps:

- Selecting an important aspect that needs to be documented
- Defining a way to characterize it
- Applying this classification scheme to all the items (or at least a representative subset of them)

- Identifying where this doesn't work and using this understanding to refine the description, classification and relationships

This will be clearer if it is applied to a real case.

Suppose, for example, that it becomes apparent that within an international business different countries employ data in distinct ways. One way to clarify this would be to use the country names to label the different approaches. But which country names should be used? Should the London office be classified as being in "England"? Probably not, the important thing is that both the London and Belfast office have the same legal constraints, and Belfast is not in England. In this case we could employ ISO3166[28], however this rather confusingly provides a code of "GB" for the long name "United Kingdom". Strictly speaking, of course, Belfast is not in "Great Britain" (which is the name of a particular island off Europe) but it is in the "United Kingdom". For the purpose of clarifying data use it might also be that the "country" being defined might need to differentiate between say "Alaska" and "USA", since Houston and Anchorage have different histories.

The crucial lesson is that although the first guess is that applying the standard would provide a reasonable list of countries our goal here is not to adhere strictly to a broad understanding of the United Nations charter but rather to understand how the business is impacted by regional differences. Clearly stating the purpose of a classification and widely circulating the list of acceptable values is more important than getting into arguments about exact definitions.

---

[28] The International Standards Organisation standard 3166 defines codes for the names of countries

Continent	Country	Region	City
Americas	USA	Alaska	Anchorage
		Continental	Houston
Europe	UK	England	London
		Scotland	Aberdeen
		Ireland	Belfast
	Denmark		Copenhagen
	Germany	East	Berlin
		West	Hamburg
	Australia		Perth

Figure 95: A scheme for defining four levels of locations

If this approach is taken then the focus will be on consistently defining a list of valid values. In the figure above there are four levels of classification, from the list of valid "Continents" to the "City" that each office is located within. Having a clearly defined list of the aspects ("Continent", "Country", "Region" and "City" in this case) and the valid values for each will move the discussion forward, allowing the participants to focus on what is important (the differences between locations).

Once a list of approved values has been selected for a particular topic the next step is to attempt to apply them to the documents to be tagged. This will often highlight instances that don't match any of the proposed entries, it will often also identify values that are ambiguous or unclear.

This way of classifying the acceptable values has a number of associated terms, taxonomy, cladistics, ontology and so on, while these terms each has its own unique flavor, debating the nuances of their distinctions is an activity best left to Professors of Semiotics or late night discussions.

The simple view is that each classification scheme has criteria on which it can be judged:

- **Complete:** does the list cover every valid possibility
- **Consistent:** does each valid entry have a single unambiguous value

- **Contained:** does each entry at one level have exactly one container at the next highest level and at least one at the next lower level
- **Unique:** does each entry uniquely define its level and place without requiring extra context

There are valid reasons for not enforcing some of these, in the figure the value "Australia" is not "Unique", when it is used it is unclear if a Continent, Country or Region is being discussed. The point here is that if there is a reason for breaking one of these constraints then, as long as everyone knows, that is acceptable.

There are many different reasons why inconsistent or incomplete schemes might be used. The highest quality naming schemes will usually be consistent and complete. But this often requires a careful, wide-ranging and therefore expensive creation process, for example by retaining specialists to interview stakeholders, gather, sift and consolidate the potential values and test against the real world. For some uses this cost can be justified, but there are many occasions where a cheaper alternative must be adopted.

An alternative that has proved attractive where a cheaper approach is required is to allow the users to add their own terms. These "folksonomies" have proved effective on many web sites, where the range of contributors makes a more formal method impossible. The results almost inevitably create sets of tags that are incomplete, inconsistent and have clear omissions, sometimes this is the only viable approach.

Defining Tags

As has already been discussed, any document management system can be thought of as a collection of files each of which has a number of "tags". These tags might be indicated in a variety of ways:

- Tags might be held in a separate list or database
- The location within a folder hierarchy might indicate which asset or activity it belongs to
- Some file formats, such as Microsoft Word files, incorporate tags as part of their structure, for example the "last modified by" property is a tag
- Often the name of the file will be used to flag some properties, a file "well_17_15_corereport.xlsx" could be a core report for the well 17/15

For most purposes, the exact way that tags are held and discovered is of less importance than what the tags indicate and the potential values they can have.

The most important element in any document management system is identifying and clarifying the aspects that will be of most value to the users of the system. If all users need to locate documents by relating them to the reservoir they are working with then every valuable document must have a reservoir tag set and the reservoir names used should be consistent and complete.

This means that in order to succeed a document management project must:

- Identify the key aspects that users wish to employ to identify documents
- For each aspect define a list of acceptable values
- For each existing document assign a suitable value for this tag
- For each new document find a way to assign the tag

Each of these requirements can cause a document management system to fail. If the wrong set of aspects is selected the users won't be able to ask the right questions. If the list of acceptable values is incomplete, or worse, ambiguous then the identified documents won't be the ones desired. If the legacy documents are not processed then users won't be able to find them.

The most common issue is with the tagging of items as they are brought in to the system. There are some aspects that theoretically could be deduced from context, for example, the system might know that the submitting user was a production engineer and, hence, deduce that this document is probably related to the production domain. This approach has been tried by a number of tool vendors but has never yet delivered reasonable results. In general users will only invest the time needed to tag submissions if they can see that they benefit when using it, again experience has shown that this is a major hurdle.

14. Auditing Data

In the DAMA Body of Knowledge this function is called "Meta Data Management", one might ask why the name has been changed here. The reason is not particularly profound, but just one of terminology, in the oil industry there is a lack of precision about the meaning of the term "meta-data". Some people would consider the date a well was drilled as being meta-data about the well, while others would consider it to be an attribute of the well itself.

There is a clear need to track the actual data, for example, noting where it originated, when it was loaded and who has corrected it since then. Many data management solutions have attempted to address this issue by incorporating a "source" attribute on each entity, but, this is open to many different interpretations. If an LAS file containing a well log is loaded into a modeling application is the source the name of the LAS file, the petrophysical application that generated it, the petrophysicist that processed it, or the logging contractor that made the original measurements?

Most attempts to track the source of information fall down because of the distributed nature of the interpretation process. Users are reluctant to invest any time in filling in the details that would be necessary, but also there is some ambiguity about which sources are important anyway. When a static geologic model is based on: the interpretation of a 3D seismic data set; formations selected by picking well logs; a regional stratigraphic column; and, the experience of a particular interpreter, it can be challenging to summarize the process in a short piece of text.

These various difficulties mean that, at the moment, most oil companies rely on the collective memory of their staff to track the provenance of data rather than using any technical solution to address this issue.

15. Data Quality

Data quality has a significant impact on oil company corporate results. One important consideration is that poor quality data is generally more expensive to manage. A more significant impact comes from the fact that poor data leads to misunderstanding the key subsurface features and properties, this greatly increases the risk of making sub-optimal business decisions.

Tracking data quality is a crucial function in data management. Users consistently complain about the quality of data that they are forced to rely on, they also usually overestimate the reliability of their own information. Systematic measurement of quality almost always reveals more serious issues than those involved anticipate.

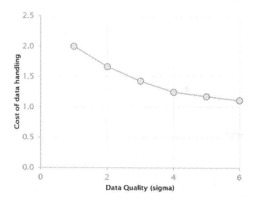

Figure 96: Data management costs drop as quality increases

The measurement and management of data quality for E&P data has become systematic and more consistently applied over the last decade. One component has been the adaption of elements of the "six sigma" approach developed for manufacturing processes. This measures data quality in terms of the rate of known defects, expressed in terms of the deviation from a normal distribution. So a defect rate of 31% would be 1 sigma, 4.6% - 2 sigma, 0.27% - 3 sigma, and so on.

Of course it is easier to agree on what constitutes a defect when considering a physical manufacturing process, with data quality the definition is less certain. Even with these challenges a number of unpublished studies have shown that the cost of handling E&P data tends to be lower as the quality increases.

Data is often moved from one repository to another, or between different versions of the same application or to a new set of users. For each of these steps it may be mapped, refined or adjusted. Over time the assumptions made evolve and new processes are applied. Each of these events causes some slight modification to the data, and generally these accumulate so that over time it becomes less "clean" and more liable to incorporate unexpected variation. This is why data quality checking is always an on-going process, never a one-time project.

Defining the business rules

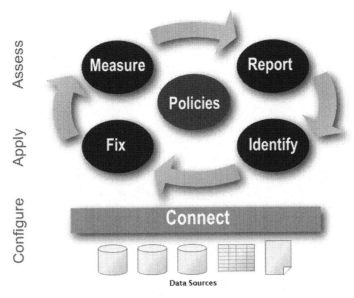

Figure 97: The elements of a quality checking system

Measurements of quality must take into account what the data is going to be used for. It is valid to apply generic tools to measure quality, but these have to exploit "rules" that are aware of the domain specific constraints and expectations. Automated quality tools tailored to E&P data sets can significantly improve data quality and have a measurable benefit through reducing overall project risk.

Any system that manages quality has to incorporate a number of components: policies that define how quality is to be measured; a mechanism that connects to the range of data sources; a scheme to identify data elements as they appear in the sources; and tools to measure, report and possibly fix any quality issues.

The policies will usually distinguish between different categories of mistakes that may exist in the data. A typical list would be:

- **Completeness:** What proportion of all the required and potential components are present
- **Consistency:** Do different ways to obtain values deliver consistent results
- **Uniqueness:** Are there multiple entries that represent the same thing
- **Currency:** Is the data available when it is needed
- **Precision:** How accurate are the measurements
- **Reasonableness:** Are the values consistent with, for example the realities of physics

Notice that this list does not include "correctness". That is because quality can only be measured by relating different data sources to each other. It is possible to quickly demonstrate when a particular piece of data is incomplete, inconsistent or unreasonable. But when no issues have yet been found there is always a chance that the next piece of additional analysis will expose some unexpected data quality concerns.

Each of these measures will be implemented by a set of rules, for example completeness policies might dictate that every well listed in one database must have a "drill plan" document in a particular shared folder. Each of the categories of rule will usually have its own schema for specifying when it is to be applied, what situation will be considered good or bad and, possibly, what automated action should take place to fix the issue.

The rules on reasonableness usually require a detailed knowledge of the domain. For example, it is common for there to be a rule for wells that the logger's total depth cannot be greater than the driller's. Often the users will already have a range of these types of checks they perform informally, they don't usually have sufficient experience to convert this understanding into the rigorous form that an automated quality tool would require. For this reason it is normal to have domain experts working with tool specialists, to define, refine and test the applied rules.

Known quality versus top quality

There is a clear distinction between documenting all the known quality issues and fixing them. Take the example of a well's location, it is not unusual for older on-shore wells to be inaccurately placed, as long as the users of that data are all aware that the position is only accurate to the nearest 100m then this will cause few issues.

The users are professionals that are aware that real data cannot ever be completely perfect, they are able to take account the limitations imposed by bad quality data if they are made aware of the glitches. It is sometimes more important to alert users of potential quality issues rather than attempting to fix them all automatically.

16. Other elements

The main focus so far has been on the "Information Layer" within E&P companies. In the discussion in chapter 7 ("Data Management Architecture") some of the other layers were mentioned.

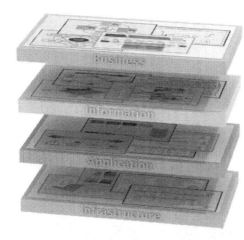

Business
  Organization, Strategy,
  Business Process

Information
  Master Data, Information Flow
  Data Relationships

Applications
  Applications Portfolio,
  Functionality

Infrastructure
  Physical Components,
  Network, Support Utilities

Figure 98: Levels of Enterprise Architecture in E&P companies

The reason for concentrating on the information layer is that this is where most of the main issues tend to be rooted. This is because the other layers tend to be better understood, the oil companies appreciate their own business processes, software vendors will fall over themselves to explain the application issues and there are available IT experts to address the infrastructure issues. There are some E&P specific infrastructure issues, after all every industry has its own challenges, but generally lessons learned in other industries apply.

This focus on the information aspects should not be taken to imply that the other elements are not important. For a solution to deliver its potential value it must coordinate a range of elements:

- **Hardware:** The necessary servers, storage, networks and workstations
- **Software:** Applications and other programs
- **Projects:** Bounded activities that integrate the proposed solution within the existing "landscape"
- **Services:** On-going processes that ensure the delivered elements continue to meet the needs
- **Information:** The appropriate data must be available and the results must be delivered
- **Business:** The results must deliver benefit by contributing to business decisions

For most situations the responsibility for implementing these aspects will be spread across different groups within the organization. The hardware might be delivered by the IT department, the definition of business benefits come from the end users and so on. But, if one of these has been ignored then the projects will fail to deliver the promised benefits. When projects fail it is normal for the guilty to be promoted and the search for a scapegoat to begin.

Experienced solution designers are aware of these dangers and will often obsess about the risks. If the responsibility for every dependent element can be documented at the start then it is easier to ensure that everything is being tracked. Even a data management focused project manager needs to be aware of the supporting elements to their project.

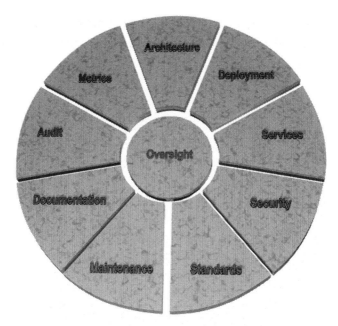

Figure 99: Ten Infrastructure & Application functions

One way to check that all the key aspects of infrastructure and applications are being covered is to use the ten "Infrastructure & Application" functions shown above.

These are similar to the ten DMBoK functions:

- **Oversight Activities:** Establishing and maintaining IT standards and policies across the organization
- **IT Architecture:** The description of the physical and logical elements of the IT environment, and to the application landscape within that environment
- **IT Deployment:** The delivery via normal project management best practices of new IT components
- **IT Services:** The delivery of IT services, usually based on the industry-standard ITIL (Information Technology Infrastructure Library) framework
- **IT Security:** Controlling access and behavior within the IT environment

- **IT Standards:** define the structure of the IT environment, including both hardware and software
- **Maintenance:** Commonly a suite of standalone processes that are executed on a regular, scheduled basis to ensure the system continues to function
- **Documentation:** Full and complete documentation must be available for all aspects of the as-built physical and logical infrastructure
- **IT Audit:** Regular audits and system tests ensure that processes and standards are being followed properly
- **Metrics:** Reporting and monitoring of performance, reliability and availability

In most cases these activities will be the responsibility of specialist groups, and the main involvement of the data management group is to validate that the needs of their proposed solution are going to be adequately met and that there is clarity about the remedial actions when it is not.

17. Assessing Data Management

In any real oil company the actual data management situation is complex and a challenge to understand. If there is a pre-existing simple description of how data flows it is almost certainly misleading and wrong. One of the essential first steps is to assess the current data management landscape, document what is currently being used, where the users are having difficulties and what they feel would be of most value to them.

Clarifying the question

There are a number of possible reasons for doing an assessment, these range from defining a coherent strategy that should be applied across a whole organization to understanding the impact that a specific new application, system or workflow will have. Obviously the first step is clearly articulating the question that the assessment is intended to clarify. Here are some typical ones:

- Define a new corporate data management strategy, vision and mission
- Describe the options for setting up a new data management department
- List the most immediate opportunities for projects to improve data handling
- Document the key data repositories currently in use and how they interact
- Propose a planned set of repositories and the change management steps required to implement them
- Identify all the systems that will be impacted by a new application
- Ascertain applications that should be retired and the activities required to replace them
- Measure the effectiveness of existing data management processes

As with any project there are three groups that should collaborate to articulate the goal: the budget holders; the users; and the project participants. The budget holders must be confident that the investment in time, effort and financial resources will be justified by the benefits to be delivered.

Setting scope

With any assessment it is important to understand the scope. Will the data to be considered include interpreted results or will it be restricted to the raw measurements? Which data domains should be covered? Is the project intended to obtain a high level overview or a detailed understanding? Is the aim to document the current situation, a near term goal or a long term vision?

The scope defines how much input must be gathered, it is not possible to understand a complete domain in detail by interviewing two or three data users, and there is little point in conducting 40 interviews about a single data category unless a very detailed picture is being sought.

Measuring Impact

A convincing business case is required to unlock funding for any improvement project. This makes the measurement of real factors in the business a crucial aspect of data management. It is possible to identify particular incidents that have had an impact on the performance of the business, but these are often specific situations that will never arise again, good indicators but anecdotal.

Identifying factors that can be translated into financial impacts on the business is actually less simple than might be thought. Users are often ingenious in finding ways to ensure that the intended consequences of company policies fail to be realized. In one Asian oil company a department manager was asked if his group was responsible for the core sample reports, his emphatic answer was that they were not. When it was pointed out that his group were the sole recipients and sent it on to the rest of the company he said

"Oh, yes everyone comes to us for it but the company standard says that the 'responsible' group must back it up and we don't have the time or systems to do that, so we aren't responsible for that data, no one is".

This type of dynamic is typical of complex systems. Often, the act of measuring something causes behavior to change so that the results don't reflect the factor that was meant to have been measured.

When a new project is initiated it is important to think about how its benefit will be proved. An example will help to illustrate the point. A project was performed to improve tracking of well log data for a national oil company. Before the project was started, a sample set of well logs was tracked for a year, and it was found that 10% of them could not be located at the end of the year. After the project's completion the same measurements were taken and the loss rate had fallen to 7%. Given the fact that this particular customer had almost 50,000 well logs this meant that an additional 1,500 well logs were available each year, at a replacement cost of $50,000 each this would represent $75M per year benefit from a project that cost $11M.

This example highlights a number of key points. First of all, the initial measurement had to be taken before the project started (in this case the first sample was measured more than a year before). Secondly, the participants in the project did not know how the samples were being selected; otherwise they would have been able to ensure the loss rate went to 0%. Thirdly, the business case must assume conservative estimates at all times, the point being that even with the most pessimistic estimates the business case is solid. Finally, when presenting to budget holders focus on financial impact, senior oil industry managers are focused on safety and financial factors, they don't usually care about wasted engineering time, or loss of irreplaceable knowledge.

Gathering data

There are four main techniques that are commonly applied during the data gathering phase:

- **Automated tools:** A piece of software is applied to the working system in order to gather measurements
- **Interviews:** Subject Matter Experts are individually quizzed about their interactions with data
- **Workshops:** Groups of experts are taken through exercises to obtain insights into the information landscape
- **Questionnaires:** A structured list of questions is delivered to a wide range of participants for them to fill out independently

The optimal balance between these approaches depends on the type of evidence that is being sought. Each technique has its own costs and strengths.

Automated tools

Automated tools are valuable when investigating detailed elements of an existing situation. Usually they will require complete access to the client's systems and are focused on gathering a particular focused set of data. It is rare that an existing tool will exactly match the important question that needs answering, so most automated tools will require some configuration and tuning to gather exactly the data this is being sought.

Interview techniques

The most detailed technique is usually the personal interview. Effective interviewing is a skill that requires practice and confidence. At the minimum the interviewer should have prepared a clear set of goals before engaging, remember that the person you are interviewing has a different job to do and will only contribute positively as long as they feel their requirements are being considered.

Usually preparing a script prior to the interviews will help smooth the process. This might be as formal as having a fixed set of questions, however that approach will often emphasize the elements that were anticipated prior to the interview rather than allowing the interviewee to highlight what they consider to be important. An unstructured general conversation would allow the subject to raise any topics they feel are important, but, without direction it might fail to touch all the questions that are important.

Generally a good compromise is to use a "check list" of topics to direct a more free flowing conversation; this will deliver insight within the interviewer's goals but also encourage the subject's contribution. Of course, this approach requires that the interviewer is knowledgeable about the topic and able to identify and explore unanticipated aspects, the level of involvement this requires means that an attentive interviewer cannot take effective notes.

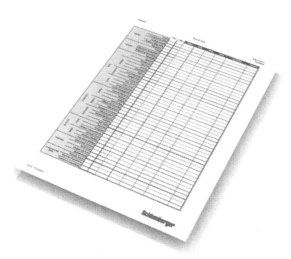

Figure 100: Physical artifacts can encourage interviewee participation

One compromise is to create a number of tables, focused on the topics to be covered, for example by drawing a table of the data categories against activities so that interviewees can identify their involvement. This ensures consistent and complete coverage with each participant. In addition, the act of taking notes on a physical version can help increase the involvement and sense of shared exploration of the contributors.

Some interviewees might be happy to have a sound recording made of their session, generally most will be wary if this is done and it will constrain their openness. Usually, it is necessary to have a separate "note taker" whose role is to transcribe the interview, again this person must be familiar with the topic. A useful approach is to have two experts as a team who alternate in the role of interviewer and note taker, this ensures that the maximum value is obtained from the interviews. This has the added advantage that the inevitable biases and blind spots that all individual experts have can be identified and discussed by the other participant during the analysis phase.

Workshops

Workshops can be a valuable way to obtain input from a number of participants at the same time. The success of the workshop will depend on two main factors: how well focused and articulated the goals are; and how well they are prepared. A good general rule is that each hour of workshop will take at least one hour of preparation time (often more) and require at least two hours of analysis and documentation.

Again it is close to impossible to both run a workshop and capture effective notes, having a second person to act as a nominated scribe is essential. Having a separate facilitator to coordinate the logistics and ensure timings are kept to is not absolutely essential but will often be a valuable addition.

Questionnaires

One might have thought that having a precise suite of questions being answered by a larger number of target users would generate the optimal response. Unfortunately this approach suffers from a range of significant shortcomings, not least the low response rates that such surveys usually deliver.

Analysis

Data that has been gathered systematically is more amenable to analysis. The main precepts of "Information Architecture" have been touched on in chapter 13 – "Document Management". Restricting collected information to particular tags will allow a number of data analysis and presentation techniques to be employed.

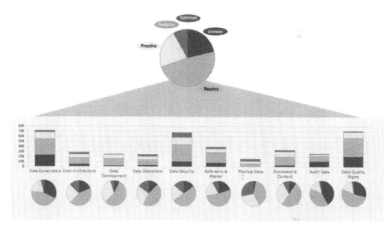

Figure 101: Contrasting maturity across different functions in an oil company

Combining different aspects helps illuminate topics. For example, in the figure above, the overall maturity of data handling is broken down by DMBoK function, this shows that in this case the "Audit Data" function is the one that needs most attention.

Presenting Results

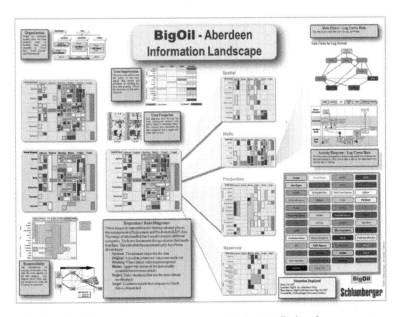

Figure 102: A poster presenting the results from a fictional assessment

The results of an assessment must be presented in a form that allows appropriate action to be taken. It does not matter if the results are presented as a poster, a detailed report or a workshop there must be a "short form" that delivers actionable suggestions and sufficient supporting material to justify the conclusions.

The most effective assessments will often start with the eventual final deliverable in mind. The form of diagrams that will most effectively convey the message determines which pieces of analysis should be performed and that, in turn, dictates the data that needs to be collected. Of course in any real assessment unanticipated themes will emerge, and there must be scope for applying new techniques and incorporating unique outputs.

18. Glossary of terms

Term	Definition
Abstraction	The creation of a common interface to data held in multiple (possibly inconsistent) sources. One of the components of the *integration spectrum*
Actor	Any participant in an *activity*, the term is used to allow discussion of the process without clarifying whether a particular contributor is a person, group or system
Activity	A process with a defined result. An activity is a lower level process than a *function*, but higher level than a task or step
Aggregation	A form of integration where the bulk of the apparent amalgamation takes place in the viewer's brain. One of the components of the *integration spectrum*
ANSI	American National Standards Institute A private not-for-profit organization that coordinates the development and use of standards in the United States and represents the needs of US stakeholders in worldwide standardization forums
API	American Petroleum Institute publishers of Oil Industry Recommended Practices
Application	A piece of software that implements functions of value to the user. Notice that an application cannot hold any data, a *Repository* holds data. Often particular repositories are named after the application that implements them.
Application Layer	The third layer of the standard *Enterprise Architecture* model. The *applications* rely on the *infrastructure layer* and provide services to the *information layer*
Approved Data	A *repository role* that only contains *data* which has passed an approval process. The term is closely related to the terms *Corporate Data*, *Master Data* and *Shared Data*
Archive Data	A *repository role*. A preserved set of data in a secondary, lower cost storage location, for infrequent reference or recovery. In *E&P IM* this *repository role* is a rarely used, because the separation of the generic infrastructure from the E&P data managers commonly makes this an issue for the IT department rather than the Petrotechnical Group
As-built	A description of what actually exists in a facility, in contrast to what is in the plans. In the oil industry the differences can be crucial
Asset	A resource which produces or may in the future produce economic benefit

Term	Definition
Asset Data Manager	The person that is accountable for data within their asset, responsible for the data quality within the asset and ensures that appropriate corrections are applied. One of the types of *data owner*
Attribute	A characteristic or property of an *entity*
Audit	A formal and official verification of validity, accuracy and conformance to requirements, regulations, standards and guidelines
Audit Data	The data that describes the processes employed to handle subsurface information. Audit Data Management is one of the extended *E&P DMBoK functions*
Audit Trail	A collection of deliverable elements that contributed to a business decision. A good audit trail will allow a later reviewer to validate the people, dates, source data and interpretations that, at the time, contributed to the decision
Budgetary Cost	The financial cost of a project, the full cost must also incorporate the *resource costs* and *opportunity costs*
Business Case	The justification for undertaking a *project* or *activity*. Usually will contrast the cost against the benefit. The benefit calculation must compare the anticipated situation if the activity is undertaken with that if it is not
Business Layer	The top layer of the standard *Enterprise Architecture* model. The business *activities* rely on the services provided by the *information layer*
Business Metric	A measurement taken to indicate the effectiveness of a business *activity*
CAIRO	An extension of a *RACI* diagram that includes the "Omitted" role
Capture	The process of identifying a potential source of data, ensuring its costs can be justified (via a VOI process) and obtaining the media that holds it. One of the steps in a typical *information lifecycle*
CDA	Common Data Access Limited. An association owned by UK based oil companies that facilitates the sharing of subsurface data between companies and with the government
Change Management	An approach to transitioning individuals, teams, and organizations from a current state to a desired future state
Chief Information Officer	CIO is a job title commonly given to the most senior executive responsible for the IT systems
Complete	A measure of *data quality*. This assesses the extent to which all anticipated elements are present

Term	Definition
Conceptual Schema	A type of *data model*, this describes a consolidated version of the *external schemas* this is consistent, but usually not complete
Consistent	A measure of *data quality*. This assesses the number of instances where multiple elements have values that conflict
Conventions	A set of high level rules that are invariably followed when a particular *data model* is being used but are not explicitly defined
Corporate Data	A *repository role* that only holds *data* which is valued by the organization. The term is closely related to the terms *Approved Data, Master Data* and *Shared Data*. Corporate Data Management is one of the *E&P* extended *DMBoK functions*. One of the typical *repository roles*
Correct	There is no way to prove that a particular piece of data is absolutely correct (although there are many ways to prove it is incorrect). Usually this is better thought of with a more specific *data quality* metric
Create	If data is generated, for example by interpretation, this can be used as a synonym for *Edit*
Currency	A measure of *data quality*. The value of *information* can depend on how long it takes to obtain it. This measure of quality assesses how timely the data is
DAMA	Data Management International. A collection of nationally based associations focused on the discipline of data management in many industries
Data	Values of qualitative or quantitative variables. Data as an abstract concept can be viewed as the lowest level of *abstraction* from which *information* and then *knowledge* are derived
Data Category	A collection of related *data* that is subject to similar processes and is maintained in closely associated *repositories*. The term data category is often applied in deliberate contrast to *data type*, since it incorporates a range of different (and often incompatible) representations
Data Consumer	A user that utilizes a particular *data category* but does not pass it on to others. The fact that data is not passed on simplifies the controls that must be applied. One of the typical *repository roles*
Data Custodian	the keepers of corporate data, responsible for ensuring the data is kept exactly as it was submitted. One of the types of *data owner*
Data Definition Owner	The authority for defining how a particular *data category* is to be handled. Commonly they will set standards, define *approval* processes and have responsibility for a related *domain*. See *Function Chief*. One of the types of *data owner*

Term	Definition
Data Development	Analysis, design, building, testing, deployment and maintenance of data management components. One of the 10 *DMBOK functions*
Data Governance	The exercise of control and strategy over *data management*. One of the 10 *DMBOK functions*
Data Model	A formal definition of the structure that holds data (the *entities*, *attributes* their relationships). Strictly the term data model can describe the *external schemas*, *conceptual schema*, *logical model* or *physical model.*, however if the term is not qualified it usually refers to the *logical model.*
Data Operations	The *services* that support *structured* data assets across the *data lifecycle*, from *capture* to *disposal*. One of the 10 *DMBOK functions*
Data Owner	The term data owner is an ambiguous one and should be avoided. More precise terms are: Data Definition Owner; DM Strategy Owner; Asset Data Manager; Operational Data Steward; Data Custodian; Document Manager; and Data User
Data Quality	A measure of the limitations that a piece of data imposes on its future use. A number of distinct types of data quality measure should be considered: *Completeness*; *Uniqueness*; *Consistency*; *Currency*; *Reasonableness*; and *Precision*. *Correctness* is not a good data quality metric. Data Quality Management is one of the 10 *DMBOK functions*
Data Security	The activities to ensure privacy and confidentiality and to prevent unauthorized and inappropriate data access, creation or change. One of the 10 *DMBOK functions*
Data Type	A classification identifying one of various types of *data*, usually within a *data model*. The term data type is often applied in deliberate contrast to the less precise term *data category* when a single representation is being implied
Data User	The users of *data*, responsible for tracking *data quality*. Typically the data user will control the *working area*. One of the types of *data owner*
Dispose	When an asset is sold the data related to it must usually be removed from all systems owned by the organization. One of the steps in a typical *information lifecycle*
Distribute	The process of sending data from the best quality source to the various *consumers*. One of the steps in a typical *information lifecycle*
DM	Data Management, see *IM*
DM Strategy Owner	The person that defines and enforces overall *data management* strategy. One of the types of *data owner*
DMBoK	The Data management Body of Knowledge: published in 2009 by *DAMA* it provides a comprehensive guide to the 10 *functions* and 7 *elements* of generic data management

Term	Definition
Document	Anything serving as a representation of a person's thinking by means of symbolic marks. In this context the term is usually applied to contrast with *structured data*, that is to indicate that the relation between this element and others is not defined. Often this is referred to as *unstructured data*
Document Management	The organizing of documents to allow users to search, identify and retrieve the files they require. This commonly involves *tagging* the *unstructured data* to classify it in a variety of ways. One of the 10 *DMBOK functions*
Document Manager	The owner of documents and other *unstructured* data. One of the types of *data owner*
Domain	See Function
E&P	Exploration & Production: the activities of an oil company focused on reserves, development and production
ECIM	Expert Centre for Information Management: an organization based in Norway that holds an annual data management meeting
Edit	When data must be corrected, interpreted or otherwise modified. This activity usually takes place in the Working Data. Often the edit step is also the stage at which new data is *created* (for example by interpreting other *data categories*). One of the steps in a typical *information lifecycle*
Element	In *DMBoK* each *function* has 7 elements: Goals & Principles; Organisation & Culture; Activities; Deliverables; Roles & Responsibilities; Practices & Techniques; and Technology.
Encoding	The lowest level of *format*, for example the way that text is represented in digital form
Energistics	*POSC* was rebranded as Energistics in 2006. A body that manages a number of standards on behalf of the oil industry
Enterprise Architecture	The discipline of documenting a business through a range of related diagrams. Often these are grouped according to the intended audience into four layers: the *business layer*; the *information layer*; the *application layer*; and the *infrastructure layer*.
Entity	A component of a *structure*, often defined within a *logical model*
Epicentre	A *logical model* that was created by *POSC* to be comprehensive for *subsurface data*
External	Data sources or destinations outside the organization
External Schemas	A type of *data model*, this describes the collected snippets from a variety of users that have distinct, often inconsistent and incomplete, impressions of the structure they require

Term	Definition
External Source	Data arriving from outside the organization. One of the typical *repository roles*
External Target	Data sent out from the organization. One of the typical *repository roles*
Format	A description of how some defined elements are to be represented in digital files. The term is ambiguous since it can refer to *encoding, structure, reference values* and *conventions*
Function	A high level group of activities, for example in some oil companies the discipline of Geophysics is seen as a function. *DMBoK* defines 10 functions of data management: Data Governance; Data Architecture; Data Development; Data Operations; Data Security; Master Data Management; Business Intelligence; Document Management; Meta Data Management; and Data Quality. For E&P data three of the functions have been modified to: Corporate Data Management; Physical Data Management; and Audit Data Management
Function Chief	Within a particular organization there will often be authorities that are leaders for particular domains, such as the Chief Petrophysicist. They will commonly be the authority for standards and workflows. See *Data Definition Owner*
Geodesy	The measurement of positions related to the Earth. The irregular nature of the planet means that locations have limits to their precision, when different elements are combined these can cause significant effects
IM	Information Management, in oil companies this term usually refers to specialists in *subsurface data* management as distinct from the *IT* group.
Information	*Data* that influences the estimated probability of an event or situation
Information Layer	The second layer of the standard *Enterprise Architecture* model. The *information* flows rely on the services provided by the *application layer* and provide facilities to the *business layer*
Information Lifecycle	An abstract listing of the *activities* carried out on *data*. Commonly may include: Capture; Load; Validate; Edit; Publish; Distribute; and Dispose
Infrastructure	The servers, networks and other computing resources
Infrastructure Layer	The most fundamental layer of the standard *Enterprise Architecture* model. The *infrastructure* provides facilities to the *application layer*
Integration Spectrum	One way to characterize approaches to integration. This divides integration techniques into: *aggregation*; *abstraction*; *transfer*; and *migration*

Term	Definition
Interpretation	The creation of a conception of the subsurface situation based on the limited evidence available. The scarcity of evidence leads to a reliance on the experience and intuition of the interpreter
IT	Information Technology. Most IT departments focus on the physical and generic information systems, leaving the subsurface information management to specialists who are often referred to as *IM* (or *DM*)
ITIL	Information Technology Infrastructure Library, a set of practices for *IT service* management
Knowledge	The systematic understanding of *information*. There is commonly said to be a hierarchy: *Data*; *Information*; Knowledge; and *Wisdom*. While there are clear definitions for the first two a precise definition of knowledge has not yet emerged and anyone that asserts that wisdom can be processed in computer systems is clearly either lying or deluded
KPI	Key Performance Indicator. A *business metric*
Load	After data has been *captured* it must be loaded into the *working area* in order to be edited. This activity is often carried out by a data specialist rather than by the data user. One of the steps in a typical *information lifecycle*
Logical Model	A type of *data model*, this describes a *structure* for the *data* that is both *consistent* and *complete* but may not provide enough detail to be implemented
Mapping	Relating one *data model* to another. This often involved the transformation of *entities* and may require the adjustment of *reference values* and *conventions*
Master Data	A *repository role* that only holds *data* which is definitive. This term is depreciated in many organizations. The term is closely related to the terms *Approved Data*, *Corporate Data* and *Shared Data*
Meta-Data	An ambiguous term, in *DAMA* it tends to be restricted to data about the processes applied, in *E&P* it also describes data that explains the information. Because of this confusion the term should be avoided.
Migration	A permanent *transfer* (and often transformation) of data to a new repository. One of the components of the *integration spectrum*.
NPD	The Norwegian Petroleum Directorate
Operational Data Steward	The custodians of data within the asset, responsible for ensuring the data is kept exactly as it was submitted. One of the types of *data owner*

Term	Definition
Opportunity Cost	Any decision to adopt a particular implementation path removes other potential routes, for example by fully employing a particular staff member they will be unable to participate in other assets
Original Data	A *repository role*, a location that stores the data exactly as it was submitted to the organization from the vendor, partner or other external source. One of the typical *repository roles*
Physical Data	Physical entities have an important role in *E&P* processes, for example core samples and seismic tapes are often kept for many years. This is a distinct element of oil company practices so is one of the *E&P* extended *DMBoK functions*
Physical Model	A type of *data model*, this describes enough detail to be able to implement a *logical model* within a particular technology
PMBoK	The Project Management Body of Knowledge published by *PMI*
PMI	Project Management Institute, a professional body that promotes *project management* and publishes the *PMBoK*. Similar to *PRINCE2*
PNEC	Petroleum Network Education Conferences, hold the largest annual *E&P data management* conference each year in Houston
POSC	The Petrotechnical Open Software Corporation. An industry body dedicated to coordinating standards for the E&P business. Was renamed as *Energistics* in 2006
PPDM	The Public Petroleum Data Model, a Calgary based initiative to define a *data model* for *subsurface data*
Precision	A measure of *data quality*. The accuracy of an *attribute*, all physical measurements are subject to limits of precision, knowing what they are (and how they impact interpretations) is an important element of data quality
PRINCE2	PRojects IN Controlled Environments 2, a *project management* methodology that encompasses the management, control and organization of a *project*. Similar to *PMI*
Programme	A collection of *projects* that are coordinated to meet a strategic need. Usually a programme will combine a shared vision and a drive towards compliance
Project	a collaborative enterprise that is planned to achieve a particular business aim under constraints in time, budget and resources. *PMI* and *PRINCE2* are two examples of project management methodologies
Project Management	The management of projects, usually employing a formal methodology such as *PRINCE2* or *PMI*

Term	Definition
Publish	After having been *edited* in the *working area* data has to be placed into the *corporate*, *approved* or *shared area*. This commonly requires review by peers and approval of the *function chief* (or their representative). One of the steps in a typical *information lifecycle*
RACI	A type of diagram used to clarify which actors are Responsible, Accountable, Consulted or Informed during a number of *activities*
Raw Data	Data that has undergone no *interpretation*. Unfortunately there is very little real raw data, most *data* elements that users perceive as raw data are someone else's *results*
Reasonable	A measure of *data quality*. Every *attribute* has a range of tests that can identify unreasonable values
Reference Data	*Data* that is used to identify other elements
Reference Values	A *complete* list of all the values which are valid for a particular *attribute* in a *data model*. This is the simplest form of *taxonomy*
Repository	A place where *data* is held. While this is most commonly used to define databases, application data stores or shared digital files it can also relate to physical items like file folders or posters on the wall
Repository Role	The roles that *repositories* are expected to play determine the *activities* that may be carried out in them and the people who are allowed to carry them out. The roles adopted will depending on which *data category* is being considered. The typical roles are: External Source; Original Data; Working Data; Corporate Data; Data Consumer; and External Target.
Resource Cost	The resources required to undertake a project, the full cost must also incorporate the *budgetary costs* and *opportunity costs*
Result	Within a single domain the naïve picture is that *raw data* comes in, is *worked* on and results go out. In fact one person's result is another person's *raw data*
SEG	Society of Exploration Geophysicists, define a number of standard formats for seismic data
Service	A continual delivery of contracted activities in response to requests, often the levels of performance will be defined by a Service Level Agreement (SLA). This term is used in contrast to a *project* which has a well-defined end point. The most widely used formalism for service delivery is *ITIL*.
Shared Data	A *repository role* that only holds *data* which is shared by many different users. The term is closely related to the terms *Approved Data*, *Corporate Data* and *Master Data*

Term	Definition
Structure	Having a clear definition of the *entities* involved and their relationships. Usually in contrast to *unstructured* data or *documents*
Subsurface Data	Data relating to the situation under the Earth's surface
Tag	A classification attached on to an existing piece of *data* in order to identify it. For example an music file might be tagged with the year of release so that users can find it later. Tagging is a key activity in *document management* and closely related to *taxonomy*
Taxonomy	A *complete*, *consistent* definition for a classification. Possibly involving more than one level
TOGAF	The Open Group Architecture Framework, a framework for enterprise architecture
Transfer	The movement of data from one *repository* to another, often involving *format* modification, *structure* transformation and value *mapping* in order to ensure it is acceptable to the target. One of the components of the *integration spectrum*
UML	Unified Modeling Language. A graphical formalism that defines a range of diagrams depicting systems, activities and behaviors
Unique	A measure of *data quality*. This aspect assesses how many items that should be unique actually occur multiple times
Unstructured	*Data* that does not conform with a *data model*, usually to contrast with *structured* data and commonly associated with *document management*
Validate	After *data* has been *loaded* into the *working area* the data user may check that there are no obvious *data quality* issues before *editing* it. One of the steps in a typical *information lifecycle*
VOI	Value of Information process, the validation of the *business case* for purchasing data by estimating the value it will deliver
Wisdom	a deep understanding and realization of *knowledge*
Working Data	One of the standard *repository roles*, the working area is usually completely under the control of the *data user*, they can do whatever they need to create results that can be *published* to the *corporate*, *approved* or *shared* repository. One of the typical *repository roles*
XML	Extensible Markup Language, a definition of how to *structure*, store, and transport data, it *encodes* data in a *format* that is both human-readable easy to parse. The standard is freely available

Term	Definition
Zachman	The Zachman Framework is a schema for organizing enterprise architecture artifacts, providing a formal and highly structured way of viewing and defining all the diagrams

19. Table of figures

The following figures are used throughout this document:

Color versions of all the figures can be found on the web site at
`http://dm4ep.com/`

20. Bibliography

There are very few books that have been written specifically about the management of data for E&P companies. That is exactly why this one was written. However there are some excellent papers that have been presented at the various specialized conferences each year and a number of good books that cover related generic topics. This selection of further reading expands the topics discussed in each of the chapters above.

The value of data to oil companies

The first paper here provided the main inspiration for this chapter, the other material supports the view that data and the way it is handled has a significant impact on the performance of oil companies.

1. *Common Data Access Limited & Schlumberger (2011)*
    "The business value case for data management" available
    for download from the web at
    http://www.oilandgasuk.co.uk/datamanagementvaluestudy/

2. *Haines, P. & Wiseman, M. (2011) "Quantitative Value of*
    Data & Data Management" presented at PNEC 15

3. *Kozman, J.B. (2005) 'Data on Demand: The Emerging*
    Business Case' SPE93625 presented at 14th SPE Middle
    East Oil & Gas Show and Conference

4. *Kozman, J.B. (2008) 'The Value of Data in Multiple*
    Repositories' SPE118451 presented at SPE Gulf Coast
    Section Digital Energy Conference and Exhibition

5. *Smith, A.H. (2002) 'The Economic Advantages of*
    Managing Data, ONCE!' SPE78337 presented at the SPE
    European Petroleum Conference

6. *Porter, M. (1985) "Competitive Advantage"*

7. Dunn, M.D. (1992) 'A Method To Estimate the Value of Well Log Information' SPE24672 presented at the SPE Annual Technical Conference and Exhibition

8. Shearer, D. & Garcia, D. (2006) "Burlington: Improving technology investment planning with metering" Presented at PNEC conference Houston

E&P data for the non-specialist

There are many excellent books and courses in geoscience, here are a few that can take you much further than the brief outline in this chapter.

9. Selley, R. (1998) "Elements of Petroleum Geology"

10. Lowrie, W. (2007) "Fundamentals of Geophysics"

11. Monroe, J. S. (2012) "Changing Earth: Exploring Geology and Evolution"

12. Murck, B. (2012) "Visualizing Geology"

Current practice

The way that real oil companies manage their data is often hard to discover.   There have been a number of presentations at conferences that provide individual insights.

13. Foreman, R. & Stone, M. (2012) "Data Management: A Strategy for the Long Haul" presented at PNEC 16

14. Priest, M. Ali, F. & Baghazal, M. (2011) "Building Sustainable Information & Knowledge Management Processes at RasGas" presented at PNEC 15

15. Kozman, J. & Hawtin, S. (2008) "The Main Sequence: Matching Data Management Change to the Organization" presented at PNEC 12

16. Garbarini, M., Catron R.E. and Pugh, R. (2008) 'Improvements in the Management of Structured and Unstructured Data' IPTC12035 presented at the International Petroleum Technology Conference 2008

17. *Marechal, A. and Robert, A. (1998) 'The Road to Information Management in the Oil Industry' from 15th World Petroleum Congress*

18. *Miller, R.G. and Gardner, J.S. (1995) 'Geoscience data value, cost and management in the oil industry' in Geological Society, London, Special Publications 1995*

The Data Management Body of Knowledge

The books from DAMA provide a wealth of detail about this topic.

19. *DAMA International (2009) "The DAMA Guide to the Data Management Body of Knowledge"*

20. *DAMA International (2008) "The DAMA Dictionary of Data Management"*

21. *Hawtin, S. (2010) "Applying DAMA to E&P Data" presented at PNEC 14, ECIM 2010 & EAGE Vienna 2011*

Data Governance

The topic of data governance has not been particularly well documented, there are many oil companies that know they need it but are uncertain about exactly what it is. Here are a number of good sources of information on the general topics covered by this chapter.

22. *The Cabinet Office (2011) "Managing Successful Programmes Manual"*

23. *PMi (2008) "The Standard for Program Management"*

24. *ISACA (2012) "COBIT 5: A Business Framework for the Governance and Management of Enterprise IT"*

25. *Kenneth Nordstrøm et al (2011) "DONG E&P Data Ownership Model" Presented at EAGE Vienna*

26. *Berkin, J. (2012) "Developing IM professionals in Schlumberger" presented at PNEC 16*

Data Management Architecture

There are many good sources for advice on documenting the way organizations work, usually under the topic of Enterprise Architecture. Unfortunately the information flows, which are so crucial for E&P activities, are not well covered in this material, however the other layers are well represented.

27. *The Open Group (2011) "TOGAF Version 9.1"*

28. *Brooch, G. Rumbaugh, J. & Jacobson, I. (2005) "The Unified Modeling Language User Guide"*

29. *Zachman, J. (2008) "Concise Definition of the Enterprise Framework"*

30. *McCandless, D. (2010) "Information is Beautiful"*

Data Development

The creation of elements that enable data handling is mainly concerned with effective project management and software development, both of these topics are well served by a range of existing sources.

31. *Office of Government Commerce (2005) "Managing Successful Projects with PRINCE2"*

32. *PMi (2008) "A Guide to the Project Management Body of Knowledge"*

33. *Hawtin, S., Abusalbi, N., Bayne, L. and Chidwick M. (2002) 'The Data Integration Spectrum' presented at AAPG Cairo 2002*

Data Operations

The definition of data management services tends to follow the ITIL model.

34. *itSMF International (2008) "IT Service Management Based on ITIL v3"*

Data Security

There is little specific information available about the data security practices of oil companies, however there are some general texts.

> 35. *Alexander, D. Finch, A. et al (2008) "Information Security Management Principles: An ISEB Certificate"*

Corporate and project data

The roles of different repositories within the context of E&P subsurface data have not been widely discussed.

> 36. *Corbin, N. (2011) "Is all E&P Data Master Data" presented at PNEC 15*

> 37. *Hawtin, S. & Bayne, L. (2003) "Deliver Your Master Data Store" presented at SMI conference in London*

Document Management

The topic of Information Architecture which is so crucial to successful document management is still the subject of some debate.

> 38. *Hicks, J. (2009) "Users are increasing their demands for metadata: can the industry meet their expectations?" presented at PNEC13*

> 39. *Rosenfeld, L. & Morville, P. (1998) "Information Architecture"*

> 40. *Morville, P. (2005) "Ambient Findability"*

Data Quality

The impact of data quality on oil company results means that a number of authors have discussed this topic.

> 41. *Turner, N. Harvey, N. & Husband, Z. (2012) "Successfully selling the case for data quality" presented at the UK DAMA meeting*

---

42. *Curtis, T. (2009) "Business Rules & Data Quality" presented at PNEC*

43. *Radhay, R. (2008) "Facilitating Data Quality Improvement in the Oil and Gas Sector" SPE Asia Pacific Conference – Perth*

44. *Duller, P.R. (1995) 'The quality assurance of geological data' from Giles, J. R. A. (ed.) 1995, Geological Data Management, Geological Society Special Publication No 97*

Other elements

Much has been written on general IT issues.

45. *Marks, L. (2008) 'IT Doesn't Matter - Or Does It?' from SPE: Journal of Petroleum Technology Dec 2008*

46. *Internet Engineering Task Force (1969-2012) – Various Request for Comments*

Assessing Data Management

The important task of examining oil company data management as it currently exists and documenting how it should be changed has a few conference papers and magazine articles. There is a wide range of material available about general topics in data analysis but a more restricted set that is specific to the E&P domain.

47. *Hawtin, S. (2009) "E&P Data Assessments - Are They Worth the Cost?" presented at PNEC 13*

48. *Kozman, J.B. & Gimenez, L. (2004) 'Maturity Models for E&P Data and Information Management Organizations' SPE88666 presented at Abu Dhabi International Conference and Exhibition*

49. *Neri, P. (2010) 'Data Management important when choosing software' in Digital Energy Journal Dec 2010*

50. *Hawtin, S. (2006) "Experience from IM Assessments: E&P Data Management in 2006" presented at PNEC 10*

51. *Janert, P. K. (2010) "Data Analysis with Open Source Tools"*

21. Index

abstraction, 56, 90, 145, 147, 150
actor, 82, 145
Adam Smith, 23
aggregation, 89, 90, 145, 150
Alaska, 123
Amerada Hess, 14
American National Standards Institute, 94, 145
American Petroleum Institute, 94, 145
application, 15, 19, 23, 41, 47, 48, 75, 106, 128, 130, 133, 135, 137, 145, 149, 150, 153
application layer, 145, 149, 150
approved data, 145, 147, 151, 153
architect, 65, 70, 71, 72, 79
archive data, 145
as-built, 136, 145
ASCII, 30, 93, 94
assembly line, 22, 23, 84, 130
asset data manager, 55, 59, 60, 61, 62, 64, 146, 148
asset lifecycle, 21, 73
asset manager, 39, 53, 59, 61
attribute, 128, 146, 152, 153
audit, 49, 128, 136, 143, 146, 150
audit data, 49, 143, 146, 150
Australia, 125
Belfast, 123
best in class, 88
blackboard, 22, 23
boots, 15
boxes and arrows, 70, 80, 82, 102
Burlington, 13, 160
business activity, 23, 54, 72, 73, 146
business case, 6, 43, 68, 85, 138, 139, 146, 154, 159
business layer, 146, 149, 150
business metric, 41, 146, 151, 160
Cairo, 88, 162
capture, 72, 111, 142, 146, 148, 150
CDA, 6, 7, 9, 146, 159
change management, 45, 53, 58, 67, 86, 137, 146
Chief Information Officer, 97, 146
competition, 3

completeness, 131, 148
completion, 26, 44, 45, 139
conceptual schema, 94, 147, 148
consistency, 24, 54, 89, 90, 110, 131, 148
convention, 93, 95, 147
core sample, 27, 29, 48, 116, 138, 152
corporate data, 53, 55, 57, 103, 107, 109, 119, 137, 145, 147, 150, 151, 153
correctness, 131, 148
correlation, 28, 36
DAMA, 1, 2, 43, 46, 47, 48, 49, 128, 147, 148, 151, 161, 163
Dan Shearer, 13, 41, 160
data adaptor, 90, 131
data category, 25, 110, 138, 147, 148, 153
data consumer, 104, 109, 147, 153
data custodian, 35, 55, 147, 148
data definition owner, 55, 60, 74, 94, 113, 147, 148, 150
data development, 85, 88, 148, 150, 162
data governance, 47, 50, 51, 56, 58, 148, 150, 161
data integration, 88, 91, 162
Data Management, 55, 76, 148, 151
data model, 18, 77, 79, 94, 95, 147, 148, 149, 151, 152, 153, 154
data operations, 45, 96, 148, 150, 162
data ownership, 54, 55, 109, 146, 147, 148, 149, 151, 161
data quality, 56, 68, 92, 129, 130, 131, 146, 147, 148, 150, 152, 153, 154, 163, 164
data security, 98, 100, 148, 150, 163
data technician, 59, 62, 63, 64, 72, 113
data type, 77, 147, 148
data user, 53, 56, 58, 59, 62, 63, 64, 138, 148, 151, 154
Debbie Garcia, 13, 41, 160
defect rate, 129

demand management, 45
dispose, 76, 148, 150
distribute, 108, 109, 114, 148, 150
DLIS, 94
DM strategy owner, 55, 148
DMBoK, 1, 42, 43, 46, 47, 48, 49,
    50, 101, 135, 143, 146, 147, 148,
    149, 150, 152, 161
Document Management, 56, 95,
    119, 143, 148, 149, 150, 163
DONG, 55, 161
drilling, 21, 24, 25, 26, 32, 33, 34,
    61, 75, 116
dynamic model, 107
EBCDIC, 94
ECIM, 2, 42, 149, 161
edit, 113, 147, 149, 150
Egypt, 20
element, 4, 39, 47, 51, 69, 89, 93,
    95, 119, 126, 134, 149, 152
encoding, 93, 94, 149, 150
Energistics, 94, 149, 152
England, 123
enterprise architecture, 72, 73, 122,
    133, 145, 146, 149, 150, 154,
    155, 162
entity, 128, 146, 149
Epicentre, 48, 77, 149
Excel, 26, 108, 119
exploration, 1, 21, 26, 30, 75, 78,
    85, 149, 153
exploration department, 21, 26, 75
Extensible Markup Language, 94,
    154
external schemas, 94, 147, 148, 149
external source, 104, 112, 113, 150,
    152, 153
external target, 110, 150, 153
extract, transform, load, 62, 90, 91,
    92, 120
facilities, 21, 24, 33, 34, 61, 150
Financial Times, 1
folksonomy, 125
format, 91, 93, 149, 150, 154
function, 13, 18, 23, 37, 48, 49, 56,
    57, 59, 64, 84, 96, 101, 121, 128,
    129, 136, 143, 145, 147, 149,
    150, 153, 164
function chief, 59, 147, 150, 153
G. Brew, 28
GeoArabia, 28

geodesy, 150
geologist, 31, 107
geology, 24, 31, 60, 94, 160
geophysicist, 31
geophysics, 150, 160
Geoshare, 2, 94
Google, 121
Great Britain, 6, 123
Guttorm Vigeland, 55
Houston, 2, 13, 14, 36, 48, 123,
    152, 160
identifier, 24, 120
information layer, 73, 133, 145,
    146, 149, 150
information lifecycle, 76, 84, 101,
    110, 111, 146, 148, 149, 150,
    151, 153, 154
Information Technology, 42, 45,
    63, 64, 73, 96, 97, 133, 134, 135,
    136, 145, 146, 150, 151, 161,
    162, 164
infrastructure, 1, 4, 72, 73, 100,
    133, 135, 136, 145, 149, 150
infrastructure layer, 145, 149, 150
Integration Spectrum, 88, 145, 150,
    151, 154
International   Standards
    Organization, 123
International Valuation Standards
    Council, 5
interpretation, 3, 25, 31, 106, 107,
    110, 113, 119, 128, 147, 151,
    153
ITIL, 42, 45, 64, 66, 96, 135, 151,
    153, 162
Janet Hicks, 163
Jess Kozman, 36, 159, 160, 164
John Berkin, 161
John Campbell, 25
Kenneth Nordstrøm, 55, 161
knowledge, 1, 10, 17, 19, 22, 23,
    42, 43, 46, 65, 128, 132, 139,
    147, 148, 151, 154, 160, 161
KPI, 151
LAS, 128
Lester Bayne, 88, 162, 163
lifecycle, 21, 41, 65, 96, 101, 110,
    111, 115, 148
load, 59, 64, 76, 109, 112, 150, 151
logical model, 78, 94, 148, 149,
    151, 152

London, 123, 161, 163
M. Barazangi, 28
management by exception, 44, 85
mapping, 151, 154
Mark Chidwick, 88, 162
Mark Wiseman, 14, 159
master data, 48, 101, 103, 145, 147, 150, 151, 153, 163
Matt Ridley, 3
meta data, 49, 101, 128, 150
Microsoft, 126
Middle East, 7, 159
migration, 150, 151
morning meeting, 26
Najib Abusalbi, 88, 162
National Data Centre, 115
Neil McNaughton, 47
Nigel Corbin, 42, 163
normal distribution, 129
North Sea, 7, 118
Norway, 7, 149, 151
Norwegian Petroleum Directorate, 151
Office of Government Commerce, 45, 66, 162
off-shoring, 5
OilIT, 47
omelet, 4
operational data steward, 55, 148, 151
opportunity cost, 146, 152, 153
original data, 103, 105, 152, 153
outcrop, 27, 32
PageRank, 121
Paul Haines, 14, 159
Peninsula Campaign, 15
petrophysics, 28, 75, 76, 109, 128, 150
Petrotechnical Open Software Corporation, 2, 48, 77, 149, 152
Phil Crouse, 2
physical data, 48, 116, 117, 118, 150, 152
physical model, 72, 95, 148, 152
planning, 13, 26, 41, 50, 69, 70, 160
PMi, 43, 44, 85, 152, 161, 162
PNEC, 2, 13, 14, 36, 41, 48, 152, 159, 160, 161, 163, 164
PowerPoint, 119

precision, 55, 62, 96, 128, 131, 148, 150, 152
presentations, 20, 99, 119, 143, 160
pre-stack seismic, 30
PRINCE2, 43, 44, 85, 86, 152, 162
production, 1, 3, 6, 8, 9, 11, 17, 21, 32, 33, 61, 68, 78, 85, 108, 116, 127, 149
programme, 42, 51, 66, 67, 69, 152
Project, 43, 65, 152, 162
Project Management, 43, 152, 162
Project Management Body of Knowledge, 43, 152, 162
Public Petroleum Data Model, 152
Publish, 57, 76, 114, 150, 153
R. Litak, 28
RACI, 83, 146, 153
raw data, 19, 63, 153
reasonable, 44, 51, 60, 122, 123, 127, 153
Red Queen, 3
Reference Values, 55, 95, 101, 150, 151, 153
relational database, 1, 95
repository role, 76, 102, 103, 110, 111, 145, 147, 150, 151, 152, 153, 154
reservoir engineering, 26, 32
resource cost, 146, 153
RP66, 94
rubbish collector, 70
sachertorte, 121
Schlumberger, 2, 7, 159, 161
security audit, 100
SEG-D, 30
SEG-Y, 30
seismic, 24, 29, 30, 31, 32, 56, 79, 106, 110, 111, 116, 128, 152, 153
SEM, 29
semiotics, 18, 124
service catalogue, 45, 65, 97
Service Level Agreement, 45, 65, 153
shared data, 114, 145, 147, 151, 153
six sigma, 129
social engineering, 100
Society of Exploration Geophysics, 30, 153
Software Engineering Institute, 35

The Management of Oil Industry

someone else's problem, 19, 61, 153
sponsorship diagram, 87, 88
spread-sheet, 20, 23, 26, 108, 119
staging area, 112
standard sequence, 36, 37, 38, 160
static model, 32
Steve Hawtin, 48, 88, 160, 161, 162, 163, 164
structural model, 32, 106
subject matter expert, 13, 18, 59, 60, 107, 113, 119, 132, 140, 147
subsurface data, 12, 49, 85, 146, 149, 150, 152, 154, 163
Swanson Drilling Rig, 25
swim-lane diagram, 81
Syria, 28
T. Sawaf, 28
tag, 126, 127, 154
taxonomy, 124, 153, 154
TCP/IP stack, 93
timeliness, 131, 147, 148
TOGAF, 154, 162
tolerance, 44
transfer, 91, 150, 151, 154
two way time, 31
Unified Modeling Language, 82, 94, 154, 162

uniqueness, 108, 125, 154
United Kingdom, 6, 7, 43, 45, 66, 123, 146, 163
United Nations, 123
United States of America, 13, 94, 123, 145
unstructured data, 56, 120, 141, 149, 154, 160
up-scale, 32
US Geological Survey, 28, 30
validate, 76, 89, 103, 113, 136, 146, 150, 154
valuation, 8
value chain, 21, 22, 74, 75, 84
Value of Information, 146, 154
Velocity Seismic Profile, 24
Vienna, 55, 121, 161
web portal, 89
web site, 170
well file, 27
well logs, 24, 26, 27, 28, 56, 75, 109, 117, 118, 128, 139, 160
Wellington, 15
wisdom, 151, 154
WITS, 94
working data, 19, 106, 108, 113, 148, 149, 151, 153, 154
Zachman Framework, 84, 155, 162

22. Further information

http://dm4ep.com/

A web site has been created at the address above to provide supplementary material of value to readers of this book (and hopefully also to other oil industry data professionals).

On it you will find:

- Downloadable color versions of all the figures
- Links to many of the papers and presentations in the bibliography
- Listings of more recent relevant papers that readers may find valuable
- Updates and corrections to the text
- Information about up-coming events relevant to oil industry data management
- Additional articles exploring some of the topics in further detail

44200819R00099

Made in the USA
Lexington, KY
25 August 2015